My Journey
to
Heaven

My Journey *to* Heaven

What I Saw and How It Changed My Life

MARVIN J. BESTEMAN

with LORILEE CRAKER

a division of Baker Publishing Group
Grand Rapids, Michigan

Published by Revell
a division of Baker Publishing Group
P.O. Box 6287, Grand Rapids, MI 49516–6287
www.revellbooks.com

Printed in the United States of America

Library of Congress Cataloging-in-Publication Data
Besteman, Marvin J., 1934–2012
    My journey to heaven : what I saw and how it changed my life / Marvin J. Besteman with Lorilee Craker.
       p. cm.
    ISBN 978-0-8007-2122-0 (pbk.)
    1. Besteman, Marvin J., 1934–2012. 2. Heaven—Christianity. 3. Near-death experiences—Religious aspects—Christianity. I. Craker, Lorilee. II. Title.
BT846.3.B47 2012
236'.24—dc23   2012015812

Published in association with the literary agency of Fedd & Company, Inc.

18 19 20   14 13

Dedicated to

Ruth,
my wife of fifty-four adventurous years

Steve Yasick,
my dear son-in-law,
who went to be with his Lord in 2006

Irvin Zylstra,
my friend since childhood,
who went to be with his Lord in July 2011

Contents

Acknowledgments

My pastor, Cal Compagner, who helped me with this major project. He and I share a loyalty to the University of Michigan football team.

My dear children, Joe and Julie Wendth, Amy Yasick, Mark and Susan Besteman. My five grandchildren.

My brothers and their wives, Ron and MaryLou and Ken and MaryLou Besteman. My brother-in-law and sister-in-law, Bill and Rose Kalkman.

My co-writer, Lorilee Craker, who inspired me when words failed me.

A special thanks to my friends at "Coffee Break," who encouraged me when I would get discouraged.

The entire staff of Revell—Vicki Crumpton, Twila Bennett, Janelle Mahlman, Barb Barnes—who were instrumental in making this book a reality.

My literary agent, Esther Fedorkevich, who guided me through the maze of the literary world.

Special friends through the years, Ken and Joyce Ball, and our skiing buddies, Ed and Jo Westenbroek.

My special Christian friends who traveled through the education world and far beyond with me. Marlan Arnoys, Roger Boerema, Herb DeJonge, Marv Huizenga, Tom O'Hara, Norm Roobol, Jack Smant, and Irv Zylstra. Their wives have also played a major role in my life.

My thanks to a special group of friends who believed in and encouraged this project from the start.

Introduction

It's been six years since I had a life-changing preview of eternity, visiting heaven's gate for about half an hour, give or take.

In that short round-trip, I was reunited with loved ones; saw babies, children, and angels; peeked at the throne of God and Book of Life; and had a conversation with the apostle Peter, who I must say was a little bit shaggy looking. He always has been my favorite character in the Bible.

At first, I promised myself that no one would ever know what had happened to me. *I* knew that it was true, and that it hadn't been a dream or a hallucination. But I felt others would question my sanity if I told them what I saw and experienced on the other side. And when you get to be my age, you don't need any more excuses for people to question your sanity.

Why would anyone believe me? I asked myself. So by and large, I kept quiet, stewing like a stubborn old goat about why I had to be sent back.

Then one day God gave me a good shove in the pants, basically telling me to open my mouth and start talking. Yes, he spoke to me out loud, and though he didn't add "or else," I didn't want to push my luck. Obviously, God wanted me to tell others about his heaven.

Soon after, I began sharing my story with grief groups, church groups, and individuals young and old.

My spiritual mentors, including my pastor, felt that about 20 percent of the people who heard my story wouldn't believe it—such is human nature and people's tendency to be cynical in the face of anything unverifiable. But in reality, it's been more like 2 percent.

Maybe that's because people can tell I'm not the kind of man to put up with a lot of malarkey. I'm a Dutchman, which means I put up with even less bunk than most. I'm a veteran of the United States Army, having served for four years in the late fifties and early sixties. I was in active duty from 1956 until 1958, and then reserve duty until 1962.

Plus, I'm a banker by trade, someone who likes to deal in concrete numbers and percentages.

So, yes, most folks have believed my story, for which I am most grateful. Oh, a few here and there chalk it up to my being at a ripe old age—"Old Marv slipped a gear or two when he dreamed this one up"—but the truth is, I'm old, but I still have all my marbles (although, don't ask my wife Ruth about that; she might change that to "most of his marbles"!).

I hope you believe me, but even if you don't, I am under orders to tell you what happened to me on the night of April 28, 2006, when God gave this grandpa a bonus, a preview of heaven beyond anything I could have dreamed up in my banker's head.

And he who commanded me to tell my story—well, I believe he thought of you personally reading this book, and how my story would fill you with wonder and give you the comfort and assurance you've been wanting all along.

At Heaven's Gate

In the middle of the night, as I lay in my hospital bed in Ann Arbor, Michigan, visions of celestial beauty were the last thing on my mind. At seventy-one, I had just had surgery at the University of Michigan Medical Center to remove a rare pancreatic tumor called *insulinoma*. It was after visiting hours, and Ruth and my family had left for the day. I was alone and racked with pain and more than a little bit grumpy as I tossed and turned; more than anything, I just wanted to sleep and escape the misery and discomfort for just a little while. I had no idea I was about to get an escape beyond my wildest dreams.

Suddenly, two men I had never seen before in my life walked into my hospital room. Don't ask me how I knew, but immediately I had a sense that these men were angels. I wasn't the least bit anxious, either.

Once they had detached me from my tangle of tubes, the angels gathered me in their arms and we began to ascend, on a quick journey that felt light and smooth through the bluest of blue skies.

I was deposited on solid ground, in front of a monumental gate. And no, I don't remember it as being "pearly."

Standing in a short line of people, I observed the other thirty-five or so heavenly travelers, people of all nationalities. Some were dressed in what I thought were probably the native costumes of their lands. One man carried a baby in his arms.

I saw color-bursts that lit up the sky, way beyond the northern lights I had seen once on a trip to Alaska. Simply glorious.

My geezer body felt young and strong and fantastic. The aches and pains and limitations of age were just gone. I felt like a teenager again, only better.

The music I heard was incomparable to anything I had ever heard before. There was a choir of a million people, thousands of organs, thousands of pianos. It was the most lush and beautiful music I had ever heard. And do you know that every single day since my experience I have heard a few snatches of that music? I am so blessed to remember that heavenly sound.

And then, a greeting: "Hello, Marv. Welcome to heaven. My name is Peter."

Standing before me was one of my best-loved scriptural figures, the hotheaded apostle Peter, the "rock" upon which Christ built his church and alleged gatekeeper of Glory. I think the reason why I've always felt close to Peter is because I find him so relatable. He's hotheaded and I'm hardheaded, just for starters.

We talked a bit, and even argued (guess who won?), and when I play that conversation over and over in my head, I am thrilled to have had such an encounter with one of the bravest and best men who ever walked this earth.

I'll tell you more about that incredible meeting later on, but for now, you should know that Peter leafed through the Book of Life, which was actually multiple books, looking for my name. But of course he couldn't find it; otherwise I would be in heaven now, possibly having another lively debate with Peter. He left his post at heaven's gate briefly to consult with God about what to do with me—keep me or send me home. My vote was definitely to keep me there. Surely it was on purpose, but Peter left the door to heaven open, revealing a translucent gate through which I could see inside.

What I saw beyond the gate is a kind of revelation. I believe God wants me to share it with you, so that you know some of what to expect when this life is over. I can't wait to tell you about how people were dressed in heaven, how magnificently healthy and happy they all looked, and how the countless babies and children I saw were laughing and playing. One of the biggest reasons I decided to share my story was to offer comfort to those who had lost a baby or a child. So many of you have lost a precious son or daughter, and I know exactly how deeply painful that loss is. Fifty-some years later, we still miss our baby boy, William John, who lived for just ten hours before he was taken from our arms.

I didn't get to see my son in heaven, but I know he's there and I will be with him next time I go. Because next time, I'm not coming back!

Wonderfully, I did see six loved ones beyond the gate, and I'll tell you all about how they looked and what they meant to me in chapters 9 and 10.

Several minutes passed before Peter returned with a divine dispatch: "Marv, I talked to God, and God told me to tell you that you have to go back, that he still has work for you to do on earth. He still has things for you to finish there."

But, but, but . . . ! Peter and I tussled a bit over that matter, you can be sure. Trust me when I say that once you visit heaven, you never, *ever* want to come back to earth. It's truly a place that is everything good and beautiful you can imagine, where you will feel more free and loved than you ever dreamed possible. It's really a future to eagerly await, that "home in Glory Land that outshines the sun," as the song goes.

In the end, I really didn't have much to say about whether I was staying or going. Before I could mount a rebuttal to Peter, I was sent back in the blink of an eye. Next thing I knew, I was back in my hospital bed at U of M (the University of Michigan).

Once again, I was lying flat on my back, riddled with pain and attached to a mess of tubes plugged in all over the place. I made a snap decision then and there never to reveal what I had seen and heard that stunning night.

Why would anyone believe one word? That good old salt-of-the-earth Marv Besteman was chosen, out of millions of people, to take a sneak peek at eternal paradise? I could just imagine what they'd be thinking:

"Sure, Marv hitched a ride with a couple of angels to the clouds above—cloud nine is more like it!"

"Isn't it sad? That nice Mr. Besteman was hallucinating that he argued with St. Peter—he even thinks he told Peter he was a 'hardheaded Hollander'! Well, he is hardheaded . . ."

I felt it in my bones—no one would buy it. I especially knew I could never tell anyone about seeing Steve, the son-in-law who had asked me years ago to be his dad, the bonus son I loved like he was my own boy. Steve had died just two months before I went to heaven, of Ehlers-Danlos syndrome, a cruel and despicable illness I wouldn't wish on my worst enemy. How I wanted to tell my daughter how wonderful her husband looked, how vibrant and content! But I felt at the time it would only confuse and hurt her. Her grief was still so raw.

The only problem was my trip to heaven *had* happened— and just the way I remembered it.

I couldn't stop thinking about my angels, and the radiant and peaceful place called heaven I flew to with them.

Images from that journey bombarded me: the colorbursts that lit up the sky, the hundreds and thousands of babies and children I saw, and for one twinkle in time, the glimpse I had of God's throne with two indescribable images upon it.

In my mind's eye, I could picture Peter perfectly, his bushy hair, his ancient robes, and the look in his eyes when he told me that he couldn't find my name in the Book of Life—"for today."

Would I buy a story like that myself if someone else was telling it? No, probably not, although I'll never know for sure.

"You Have Been Truly Blessed"

For a long time, I was angry at God for taking me to that perfect, joyful place and then bringing me back to life on earth, to an old man's aches and pains, in a place full of dirt and crime, disease and tears. I've since done some reading about people who have visited heaven, and by and large they almost all come back feeling depressed and angry. According to some scholars, even Lazarus, whom Jesus raised from the grave, the brother over whom Mary and Martha wept, struggled in his life after resurrection.

It's hard for people to understand, I know. Wouldn't a heavenly traveler be filled to the brim with marvelous news of things to come for all God's children? Yet, I know how much I wrestled with negative emotions when I came back. In the end, everyone who sees heaven even for one second wants to stay forever, no matter how nice their life might be here on earth.

God had plans for me, a mission for this retiree that went way beyond golfing and having coffee at Arnie's Bakery with my buddies. He had begun a work in me that night, and slowly but surely he showed me his purpose and mission in sending me on a round-trip to heaven and back.

Five months after my return, I broke down and told my sweetheart of fifty years everything. As tears poured down my face, the whole account came tumbling out, even the part about seeing our Amy's Steve.

Ruth's response changed everything.

"Marv, you have been truly blessed," she said, shaking her head, her bright blue eyes wide with wonder.

After I broke the ice with Ruth, my resolve to keep all the hard-to-believe details to myself began to melt. We shared the story with our three children, Julie, Amy, and Mark.

That Christmas, Amy gave me a copy of a book I had never heard of—*90 Minutes in Heaven* by Don Piper.

Somehow, this bestseller had completely escaped my attention until that Christmas morning after the heaven trip. It occurred to me that God might want me to write a book too. But I'm a banker, not a writer, and writing a book seemed to me then about as likely as traveling to heaven.

Then, nine months after my surgery, I was experiencing some issues with my stomach, which was swollen and distended. My visit to a doctor, the conversation we had that day in his office, and the crystal clear voice of direction I heard in my spirit sent me deeper down the path of sharing my story. Withholding what I had experienced was no longer an option.

God had made it perfectly plain: if I would faithfully tell his story, he would use it to bring comfort to the grieving, to encourage those who were dying and their loved ones, and to plant a seed of hope in those who had not yet chosen Christ.

That's why you hold my story today. I invite you to be my companion and I yours on a journey to heaven and back. Together, we'll pull back the curtain separating us from the other side, and we'll learn many intriguing and fantastic things about angels, the Book of Life, the apostle Peter, and heaven itself, where God prepares a place for you and me. At last, we will be with the Person we were made for, in a home we were made to be.

One more thing before we start: I have given many talks over the last few years to people eager for information on what heaven is like. At the end of every talk, I tell folks that next time, I won't be coming back. I'll be staying there forever with my Lord and those I love.

"And I'll be waiting for each one of you at the gate," I say as I close my talk. "Will I see you there?"

Will I see *you*? If you don't already know the answer to this question, will you do an old man a favor and chew on it as we travel through these pages together?

Okay then, let's get going . . .

1

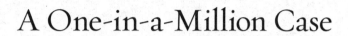

A One-in-a-Million Case

I had never heard of insulinoma before I was diagnosed with it. As diseases go, this wasn't one of the famous ones that cause people to cluck their tongues, grimace, or shake their heads in sympathy. When I told people I had insulinoma, they looked at me like they didn't know what I was talking about—which they didn't.

But, have it I did, and that's what led me to the University of Michigan Medical Center in Ann Arbor, Michigan, in April of 2006.

It all started in 2003, three years before my diagnosis with this strange illness. Ruth and I were in Florida for a few months, basking in the sun and trying to beat each other at golf (at the time, I could still beat her, but barely). It was there I had my first "episode."

Apparently (I have no memory of this), one night we were sitting around the condo, and suddenly I just zoned out. According to Ruth, I just stared into space for an hour, not knowing who she was, completely disoriented and confused, and a little bit agitated. One bonus of having a nurse for a wife is that she can often tell what's wrong with me, or at least she knows what to do to help the situation.

She thought it seemed like a case of low blood sugar, and she shoved a bit of chocolate in my mouth to get my blood sugar evened out. Ruth told me I couldn't even shut my own mouth to chew it, that's how out to lunch I was. She shut my mouth for me, something she probably wishes she could have done a long time ago.

Ruth took me to the ER for tests the next day and they couldn't find anything wrong.

For the next three years, I was fine—no more "episodes" to speak of. Since I hadn't even remembered what happened, I didn't think much about it. Ruth, though, being a nurse and my wife both, tucked it away in the back of her mind, wondering if it would ever happen again and why it happened in the first place.

We were vacationing up north in Boyne Mountain, Michigan, with two of our grandchildren, when I had another spell. It was the same kind of thing as in Florida; I woke up sometime in the night, dazed and incoherent, and had no idea who Ruth was or where I was. When Ruth woke up, she saw that I had pulled my legs up in the fetal position, and I was staring at her without really seeing her. I moaned and moaned, but didn't appear to have any pain.

Ruth got me up to go to the bathroom, and she had to hold me up the whole way because I was so shaky.

She made me eat some more chocolate, but somehow kept me quiet. Our granddaughter was sleeping in the same hotel room, and she didn't want to scare her.

The next morning, I felt perfectly fine, once again, and had no memory of anything happening the night before. We took the kids to the water park, went out for lunch, and drove home to Grand Rapids, where it happened again.

I had fallen asleep on the couch, and when I woke up, once more I didn't know where I was or who Ruth was. According to Ruth, I was acting anxious and a bit crazy, my heart racing and my limbs shaking. I was moaning again, and repeatedly beating the couch cushions.

This time, she was freaking out too, on the inside. I began crawling around on the floor, trying to get out of the condo, trying to get away from poor Ruth. She was grabbing me by the belt, attempting to physically slow me down so I couldn't get out. She finally managed to lock the doors and dial 911. Nurse or no nurse, my wife was definitely alarmed, but her training helped her stay calm and take command of the situation.

"What's he doing?" the 911 dispatcher asked her.

"He's crawling around on the floor, and he has no idea who I am."

The ambulance got there about five minutes later, loaded me up, and took me to Spectrum Health hospital in downtown Grand Rapids. I was at Spectrum for ten days, where I was poked and prodded within an inch of my life. Finally, they diagnosed me with insulinoma, a rare tumor of the pancreas that shows itself as being the exact opposite of diabetes. My pancreas was generating so much insulin it was eating all the sugar in my body, hence the strange spells. I had a blood sugar level of 31, which is apparently very bad news.

I had the dubious honor of being the first case of insulinoma they had ever diagnosed at this hospital, one of the top hospitals in the United States. Literally, less than one in one million people are diagnosed with it each year. Around 200 cases are confirmed annually in the whole country. I was one of those lucky people.

The doctors at Spectrum recommended that I see a very specialized surgeon, either at the University of Michigan Medical Center in Ann Arbor or at the Mayo Clinic in Rochester, Minnesota. I had attended U of M for a short time in my college days; I even laced up skates and played hockey for them back in the day. I figured they already had some of my money, so I might as well give them more of it.

I had to lie around and wait for a couple of days for a bed to be free in Ann Arbor. Ruth had left the hospital for the night and returned to our home, just twenty minutes away, so I was alone when abruptly I was told they had a bed ready at U of M. They packed me in an ambulance and off we sped to Ann Arbor, two and a half hours away. Ruth decided to come the next day, in the daylight, so she could find the place more easily.

Once at U of M, I found out just how special I was. There at the hospital, doctors wouldn't come in my room one at a time; it always was three to five at a time. I guess my condition was so rare the doctors were swarming me so they could inspect this extraordinary guy and his exceptional ailment.

They had diagnosed me with insulinoma in Grand Rapids, but those doctors and the new ones in Ann Arbor still didn't know exactly where the tumor was located on my pancreas.

This was crucial, because apparently a surgeon can't just go in and poke around someone's pancreas. Evidently, you can bleed terribly if they go in without knowing the exact spot they are trying to reach. But finding the right spot was turning out to be easier said than done.

A young doctor at the U of M hospital had a brilliant idea: she would pass a pediatric scope through me to find the exact location of my tumor. It worked, thanks be to God. Ruth and I were so relieved that she had found the tumor. We didn't want to face the possibility of excessive bleeding in surgery.

My surgery lasted for five hours. Dear Ruth had already been through such a roller coaster, wondering what was wrong with me, and knowing there was something way off, but not knowing what it could be. My "episodes" were stressful too, and then the drama of my being diagnosed with this extremely rare illness and the worry over whether or not the doctors would find the site of the tumor.

She says God gave her deep comfort throughout those five hours as she waited to find out how things had gone on the operating table. As it turned out, things had gone well, in terms of the doctor's goals for the surgery. They had found the site of the tumor no problem, and my blood glucose went from a low 80 to 180 and quickly to a normal 115 once the tumor was out. The only problem was that I awakened in more pain than I thought was humanly possible.

According to Ruth and our family and friends, plenty of loved ones stopped by to visit me after my surgery. But I didn't know and didn't care who was in that room. Phil Mickelson could've stopped by to get some golf tips from me, and I wouldn't have cared.

A doctor whose sole job was to control people's pain spent three hours in my hospital room, adjusting my pain medications. From about five p.m. to eight p.m. that evening, she tried to get my pain under control. Whatever she was doing wasn't working one little bit, though it wasn't for lack of her trying.

I'm not being a big baby when I tell you it was horrible. I've been told the reason why I hurt so bad is because the pancreas is behind the stomach, so the surgeon had to move my other organs around to get to it. Plus, with a major surgery like this, the nerve endings are apparently severed, and then later they have to reattach and regenerate. At that point, my nerve endings hadn't regenerated yet, to say the least. Oh, and I almost forgot: the epidural stopped working during the surgery and I had to have a new one midway through the procedure. "Ouch" doesn't begin to cover it.

Nurses like to say, "How's your pain on a scale of one to ten?" This was way beyond a ten.

I was in and out, dozing, coming to and from that fiery pain. I remember just jabbing my pain control button over and over but nothing seemed to work. Ruth says that because it was my first night, post-op, the nurses would have been in about every half an hour to check on me. Ruth wasn't familiar with Ann Arbor, and she wanted to get back to her hotel before it got too dark outside. She kissed me on the cheek, told me she loved me, and walked out of the room. She left at about eight o'clock, just after the pain control doc had given up for the night and left my room.

I lay in my bed, miserable and terribly restless with the pain. There was a clock in my room, but I couldn't see it (and I didn't care what time it was, either). That's why I didn't know exactly what time it was on the night of April 27, 2006, or early in the morning of April 28, when two strangers entered my room and I instantly forgot about all the pain.

2

Two Angels

D on't ask me how I knew the two strangers who had just walked into my hospital room were angels; I just knew they were. Beyond any doubt, these were angelic visitors, come to take me home.

I wasn't one bit worried about it, either. A feeling of deep calm washed over me as these two men approached my bed, one on either side of me. They were smiling and quiet. My angels looked like regular guys, except regular guys usually don't wear white robes. Both looked in their mid-forties and stood about 5'8" to 5'10". One had longish brown hair, and the other one had shorter hair.

Everyone has a mental picture of angels, and so did I. When I had thought of angels before I actually met one, I pictured them as younger than the beings I saw. I also thought angels were men and women both, but maybe that's just because of that old TV show, *Touched by an Angel*.

And no, actually, neither one of them had wings. (I know that's what you were wondering, because that's one of the top questions I get about my experience: Did my angels have wings?) A little while later, I did have an encounter with winged creatures, but we'll get to that part in due time.

The angels were as tender as tender could be, peaceable and silent as they unhooked me from my tubes. (I was attached to about five different tubes—IV, gastric tubes, etc.)

Now, just hold on a minute. Why would angels—with superpowers that make Spiderman and Superman look like wimps—bother to detach me from the tubes holding me to my hospital bed and this earth? Couldn't they just beam me up to heaven, like the Starship Enterprise's chief engineer, Scotty, used to propel Captain Kirk back to the ship?

Of course they *could've* beamed me up, blasted me off like a rocket, floated me like a balloon, but they didn't. My angels chose to carefully and gently unhook each and every tube before we took off, and I'm not totally sure why.

Naturally, I have some theories. They knew, because God told them, that I was a Dutchman, a retired banker, and a Midwesterner to boot. I'm a man who likes my t's crossed and my i's dotted, so perhaps they felt it best to unplug me from planet Earth in an orderly fashion.

My gut tells me they were preparing me for what would come next, easing me into transition from this life to the next.

My angels each put their arms around one side of me; then I had a sudden upward-trend feeling, and the three of us began to fly to heaven. My angels were carrying me with their arms around me. I wasn't at all afraid; just the opposite. I felt perfect serenity, yet also a sense of excitement for what was to come. It was smooth and wonderful, I can assure you, not like some commercial airline, bumping along the skies.

I couldn't say how long the trip took—a few seconds to a couple of minutes, at the most. My angels and I flew through a brilliantly blue sky, and I had a profound sense of lightness and calm.

There was just so much peace.

"Ministers of the Divine Bounty"

Before I met the two angels who came to take me to heaven, I hadn't thought too much about the topic. I knew angels were with me when I was born, and that they would be with me when I died. I had believed in angels as long as I could remember. When I met my two angels, though, and flew with them to heaven, it got me thinking later about all the ways in which angels are with us and for us, in between birth and death.

I can count on one hand the number of good, solid sermons I've heard in my lifetime on the topic of angels. When you're Dutch, you're stoic, proud of the dose of skepticism that runs through your "orange" veins (orange, for those who don't know, is the color of the Dutch Royal Family, the House of Oranje-Nassau). I'm not royalty, but I am Dutch and proud of it. What I'm trying to say is that Dutch Calvinists aren't normally too big on angel sightings.

Even John Calvin, who founded reformed theology, was cautious in discussing the topic of angels. Too much talk of angels, he once said, is apart from the Bible, and therefore not verifiable. (Good thing Calvin wasn't around in the mid-1990s, when angels were all the rage and there seemed to be fluffy, chubby heavenly beings floating behind every bush.)

But even Calvin, with his reluctance to fall into the silliness that can occur when people obsess about angels, said they are "ministers and dispensers of the divine bounty towards us."

There's no doubt the way my angels picked me up in my hospital room, with all the respect and kindness in this world and the next, why, that was a kind of "bounty," or gift, to me.

I bet Lazarus felt the same way, when angels carried him to "Abraham's bosom" in the parable of the poor man and the rich man in Luke 16:22: "Now the poor man died and was carried away by the angels to Abraham's bosom; and the rich man also died and was buried" (NASB). Caring for believers at the moment of death is just one of the many jobs angels fill, according to the Bible.

I always knew, since Sunday School days, that angels were workers of Christ, like Christ, watching over what we say and do.

After my time in heaven, I was much more fascinated with angels than ever before, and I decided to study the Bible and find out as much as I could about the two strangers who entered my hospital room and their fellow beings. Plus, after sharing my heaven story with others, folks started telling me their own incredible angel stories, some of which I will pass on to you.

But first, may I share with you some of the fantastic things I learned about angels in the Bible? I think you'll be as intrigued as I am.

Angels 101

- **Angels are referred to 196 times in Scripture,** 103 times in the Old Testament and 93 times in the New

Testament. These references are scattered throughout the Bible in at least 34 books from Genesis to Revelation.

- **Angels are celestial messengers.** The Hebrew word for angel is *mal'ach*, and the Greek word is *angelos*. Both words mean "messenger" and describe one who carries out the goals and commands of the One they serve.
- **Angels were created *before* the earth.** In the book of Job, when God is questioning Job, we are told that angels were already there when the earth was created:

> Where were you when I created the earth?
> Tell me, since you know so much!
> Who decided on its size? Certainly you'll know that!
> Who came up with the blueprints and measurements?
> How was its foundation poured,
> and who set the cornerstone,
> While the morning stars sang in chorus
> and *all the angels shouted praise?*
> Job 38:4–7 Message

- **Angels live in heaven but can travel anywhere in the cosmos and creation.** In the book of Mark, Jesus spoke of "the angels in heaven," which strongly suggests that angels have a home or center there for their activities. However, they have many missions to accomplish, and therefore have access to the entire universe, both heaven and earth. In the Bible, angels have served on earth, as in the case of the angel who flew in and brought Daniel an answer to his prayer, and in heaven: four angels described in Revelation stood at the four corners of earth, "standing steady with a firm grip on the four winds so no wind would blow on earth or sea, not even rustle a tree." From the Milky Way to Milwaukee, from the throne of God to the porch swings of earth—angels have access to the whole universe.

- **Angels are superheroes.** But make no mistake, they are not as powerful as God. In fact, the Bible tells us they are limited. Still, compared to us humans, angels are much smarter and wiser and possess astounding powers. For starters, they can fly, with or without wings (remember, my angels were wingless), and they can turn into a human or heavenly being in the twinkling of an eye. But so often, as the stories later in this chapter illustrate, angels can show up at any time, and then vanish into thin air. They are incredibly strong too. The stone covering Jesus's tomb, for example, weighed an estimated 1,000 to 2,000 pounds, the same heft as a midsize car. An angel rolled it away like it was a bowling ball. In Acts, an angel broke into a jail, snapped iron chains with his bare hands, and let the imprisoned apostles go free. The apostle Peter says it all: Angels are our "superiors in every way" (2 Peter 2:11 Message).

- **Angels are on a mission.** Their main job seems to be worshiping and praising God in heaven (I heard their phenomenal voices when I was at the gate). But angels also reveal God's will to his children, like the angel Gabriel revealed to Mary that she would be with child. They guide and instruct us, giving instructions to Joseph, the women at the tomb, Philip, Cornelius, and many others in the Bible. God used angels to provide

36

physical needs such as food and water for Hagar, Elijah, and Christ after his temptation. They protect us, keeping us out of physical danger—like they protected Daniel in the lions' den—and deliver us from danger once we're in it. Last but not least, one of the angelic duties is to strengthen and encourage us, such as the way an angel encouraged Paul in Acts 27 by telling him that he and everyone else on the ship would survive the impending shipwreck.

- **Angels are spoken of as men in the Bible.** Now, I know in Christ there is no "male or female." Both men and women are made in his image and he loves them equally. My angels were men, and so are the vast majority of angels mentioned in the Bible, at least the ones that took on the appearance of humans. Of course, it's possible that since angels are spirit beings, they can take on the appearance of women, as well as men (see Gordy's story below). There is one exception in the Bible, in the book of Zechariah, that contains a clue that there might be female angels: "Then lifted I up mine eyes, and looked, and, behold, there came out two women, and the wind was in their wings; for they had wings like the wings of a stork" (Zech. 5:9 KJV). A stork, huh? Now that hit a nerve for me, for reasons I'll get to in just a bit. Anyway, it's possible this verse lends some credibility to the existence of female angels. Some theologians think the winged women here are indeed celestial beings, but not necessarily angels. I'll let them work out the fine tuning on that particular point.

- **Angels are invisible, unless God opens our eyes to them or they take on the appearance of real men.** Since they are spirit beings, we usually can't see the angels that are here with us, taking care of us, ministering to us, and fighting on our behalf. But sometimes God gives us the ability to see them, like I was lucky enough to do. Balaam, the donkey man, could not see the angel standing in his way until the Lord opened his eyes (Num. 22:31), and Elisha's servant was blind to the crowd of angels surrounding him until Elisha prayed for his eyes to be opened (2 Kings 6:17). Over and over again in Scripture, angels were mistaken for men because so often they looked exactly like men! Abraham thought the three angels who approached his tent in the desert were regular visitors, and he offered them food and drink. His nephew Lot thought the same thing when, soon after his uncle's angelic encounter, two angels showed up at his house in Sodom. He invited the angels to wash their feet and stay the night. I don't think he would have thought of clean feet if they didn't look like regular men.

My angels looked like men I might see on the golf course, or at a hockey game, except of course they were wearing long-sleeved robes. Their clothes were white and gauzy, almost filmy, but not quite see-through, and they hung about two or three inches from the floor. Both angels wore ropes or long rags belted around their waists.

Angels are sometimes described in the Bible as having faces like "lightning" and wearing blazing white, dazzling "raiment," which is a ten-dollar word for clothing. At the sight of those angels, people fell on their faces in fear and wonder.

Angels Unaware

After my trip to heaven, I marveled at how many times in my life I must have been surrounded by angels and hadn't known it. How often had I been teeing off on the same golf green as an angel, or sitting next to an angel at a hockey game, strangers who look and act as normal as can be?

So many people have asked me about what my angels were like, and some have even told me their own stories of encountering angels here on earth. I picked several of these stories to share with you, hoping and praying you'll be as captivated, inspired, and encouraged as I was by them.

Janet's Angel

Janet was the kind of lady people didn't even see. Awkwardly lacking in social graces, Janet seemed to be about as unimportant a person as you could possibly imagine.

A worker on the assembly line of a cookie factory, Janet went home each night to a cramped and dingy apartment, where she would call her elderly mother, Millie, to chat, or else turn on the TV and heat up a frozen meal of some kind. Her life was about as dull as you could imagine.

But God, her heavenly Father, loved her so much that he would send an angel to her funeral to deliver a message so powerful that the handful of attendees would never forget it.

One day, when Janet was just in her late forties, she died suddenly of a massive heart attack. With few friends and even fewer family members, it fell to the members of her mother's church small group to plan the funeral of a woman they barely knew.

For Millie's sake, the small group members tried to make Janet's funeral nice and meaningful. They ordered purple flowers for the service, because Millie told them it was Janet's favorite color. Her best-loved songs were sung by a sparse crowd of about thirty people who dribbled into the five-hundred-seat sanctuary. The apples of Janet's eye—her two little grand-nieces—cuddled up to their mother and great-grandmother in the front pew, nearly empty except for the four of them.

It was a risk, but Millie had responded favorably when asked if she thought there should be time given for people to share their memories of Janet. Their worst fears—that no one would walk up to the microphone with a memory—almost came true as an awkward silence fell over the small crowd.

Just as the pastor began to clear his throat to bring the dismal sharing time to a close, a young African-American man seated in a side pew, several rows from everyone else, stood up.

"I have a message," he said in a clear, strong voice that rang out like a bell. The young man was wearing a green T-shirt with three crosses on it. With deep conviction, he began to read from Hebrews 12, starting in verse 22:

> But you have come to Mount Zion, to the heavenly Jerusalem, the city of the living God. You have come to thousands upon thousands of angels in joyful assembly, to the church of the firstborn, whose names are written in heaven. You have come to God, the judge of all men, to the spirits of righteous men made perfect. (vv. 22–23 NIV'84)

The man with the crosses on his shirt continued to read the passage, with perfect clarity and a resounding, authoritative tone. Janet's family stared at him; they had never laid eyes on him before and they were fairly sure Janet hadn't either. The pastor and head elder began to trade glances with each other. With over thirty years in ministry together, they could just about read each other's minds. *Who is this guy? Let's check him out when the service is over.* They nodded at each other in understanding as the man's voice got even more booming and decisive as he got to the last verses in the chapter:

> Therefore, since we are receiving a kingdom that cannot be shaken, let us be thankful, and so worship God accept- ably with reverence and awe, for our *"God is a consuming fire."* (vv. 28–29 NIV'84)

The young man was almost shouting as he delivered the last words of the passage, "Our God is a consuming fire." He closed his Bible and quietly took his seat as the stunned members of the congregation gawked at him. Was he a friend of Janet's? If so, he wasn't sitting with the handful of co-workers and other acquaintances. Several curious attendees made a mental note to meet the mysterious man after the service was done, and they turned their attention to the front and the pastor's sermon.

But when the service ended, and Millie and her tiny family trooped down the aisle to the church foyer, with the other attendees following suit, the young man was nowhere to be seen. Had he slipped out sometime during the pastor's sermon? The head elder, seated up on the stage at the front of the church, had been keeping a close eye on the man. He never saw him leave. In fact, no one remembered seeing the man leave, even though at least a dozen people had a clear view of him from across the church.

It was strange, but then again, Madison Square Church is situated in the inner city, and they have had their share of odd visitors come in off the street over the years. Besides, there was Janet's family to comfort, and a funeral lunch to partake of. Most people forgot about it for the time being, but not the pastor or the head elder.

Both of them knew very well that this stranger was unlike any they had ever received in all their years of ministry. He was clearly sober, tidy (if oddly dressed for a funeral), and completely in command of his speech and delivery. It was as if he had a message to deliver, a message on behalf of someone else.

"Our God is a consuming fire."

How bold and commanding his voice had been as he read those words from Hebrews 12! The pastor stole away to a quiet room and opened his Bible to Hebrews 12, rereading the passage the visitor had delivered so compellingly. What an unlikely message to be delivered at a funeral, especially for a funeral of one as meek and mild as Janet. Yet somehow, the pastor and everyone gathered there felt the fiery missive was oddly fitting. The takeaway seemed to be that Janet may have lived a quiet life, nearly unnoticeable to all but a few loved ones, yet she believed in the God of "consuming fire," and was with him now in heaven. Her choice, to believe in this God, had been brash and daring—everything she seemed not to be—and it meant that Janet had now joined "thousands upon thousands of angels in joyful assembly."

Speaking of angels, the pastor's suspicion was growing. How had their eagle-eyed head elder, who never missed a single thing, missed the young man's leaving the sanctuary? For that matter, how had *everyone* missed his leaving?

The pastor read every word of the Hebrews passage carefully, praying for wisdom to receive the message in the way God had intended. He came to where the young man had stopped, and instead of ending there, he decided to keep reading, hoping to gain some context for the passage.

A chill ran up his spine as the pastor took in the very next passage following the stranger's reading: "Keep on loving each other as brothers. *Do not forget to entertain strangers, for by so doing some people have entertained angels without knowing it*" (Heb. 13:1–2 NIV'84).

Though there was no proof this stranger was an angel (there never is, by the way), the pastor felt a wave of gratitude wash over him. He felt sure that he and the small crowd of mourners at the funeral had entertained an angel without knowing it. They had been reminded by this heavenly messenger in no uncertain terms of God's overwhelming, all-consuming holiness.

And no one who attended the humble funeral of lonely, unimportant Janet ever thought about her in the same way again, nor did they forget that they had been visited by an angel in a green T-shirt.

"My Name Is Otis"

Janet's angel was on a mission to deliver a message from God, but some of the angel stories people have told me revolve around other purposes. Just as God used angels to supply water for Hagar's thirsty little boy, a cake baked on coals for a hungry Elijah as he hid in the wilderness, and sustenance for Jesus after his temptation, angels are all around us, helping us in often very practical ways. Jamie's story features a hands-on angel called Otis, who couldn't be more down-to-earth.

Jamie is a bubbly young mother from Texas, and she shared three stories of how she believes God had sent angels to watch over and rescue her and her loved ones.

When I was little, I was traveling with my grandparents on a camping trip, when we had some car trouble. My granddad pulled the camper over and looked under the hood of the truck to see what was going on. A man stopped his car and offered to help. He and Granddad looked under the hood together and worked on the engine for quite a while, chatting as they worked. When Granddad followed the man to get something out of the trunk of the man's car, Granddad noticed some fishing gear in there and asked him about it. The man said he and his brothers were fishermen. It seemed odd, because we were nowhere near a body of water big enough to fish commercially.

My grandmother is Southern, and Southern ladies write thank-you notes for all occasions. She tried to get him to write down his address for her so she could send him a thank-you note. The man politely refused. Grandma and Granddad offered to pay him, but he wouldn't accept a thing or give them any information. "At least let us take you out to eat," Grandpa begged him, but the stranger just smiled and said that wasn't necessary, that he was glad to help them. "My name is Otis," he said, when my grandparents asked for his name (Grandma was probably hoping for a last name so she could look him up and send that darn thank-you card anyway!). But he didn't give a last name and they didn't want to push him. Otis followed us in his car, a good bit out of his way, to a dealership where he knew we could get fixed up. He waved to us as he drove on by, and we never saw him again.

Agents of Rescue

Like the mysterious "fourth man" who rescued Shadrach, Meshach, and Abednego from the blazing furnace in Daniel 3, angels are sent out to liberate us from grave danger. King Nebuchadnezzar and his astonished entourage actually saw the rescuing angel, who looked like "a son of the gods" (v. 25), standing in the fire, cool as can be, with the trio of men the king had supposed he had sent to their deaths. But so often, we don't see anyone at all, as the angels who save us from harm are invisible, or maybe just manifested as a flash of light. This was true in Jamie's other stories, the first of which happened to a friend of hers, and the second hit her very close to home.

Missy's Story

"A friend's dad always specifically prayed for his children's protection every time they left the house. On this occasion, he prayed for Missy to be safe on the road before a particular trip. She was driving behind an 18-wheeler, and she saw a flash of light. Her car suddenly died, stopping right in the middle of the road and she watched as the semitruck pulled away from her, swerving wildly as it had had a tire blowout! She knew if her car had not stopped right there at that specific spot on the road, there would have been no way she could have avoided colliding with the semi. There was nothing wrong with the car, before or after it died, and it started right up again as if nothing had happened. She believes her dad's prayers were answered and an angel protected her that day."

Zackary's Story

"Last summer we were at a benefit golf tournament and our one-year-old son, Zackary, was run over by a 700-pound golf cart, driven by an 8-year-old with no adult supervising him. I didn't see it happen as I had turned my back for just a few seconds and was talking to someone. I heard screaming and turned around to see my baby boy under the golf cart. My heart stopped, of course. I have never been more terrified in my life. Someone called 911 and a bunch of men tried to pull him from underneath the cart. When they finally pulled him out, I frantically checked him out, and to my profound relief Zackary only had a few light abrasions on his neck and cheek, and a small scrape on his head. Later, the medics and doctors couldn't believe he had not been seriously injured or killed. One of them said to me that there was just no explanation for it other than an angel had put himself between my baby and the golf cart and saved him."

Just for good measure, and because I want you to go away from this chapter with your eyes wide open to the possibility of angels working in our midst, I want to share two more tales, passed on to me by others full of wonder at what they had experienced.

Sharon's Story

"My girlfriend and I were at a work-related conference in Philadelphia and we went into the city one night for dinner. We didn't realize how late it was getting, and when we finally paid our bill and went out to our rental car, the parking lot was deserted except for one other car across the lot.

"Two guys were standing over by the car, watching us intently, and it seemed to me, in a predatory way. I had a creepy feeling about them and the whole situation. I felt so vulnerable at that moment. Suddenly, the two guys were joined by about eight other men, wearing white robes, who surrounded the two men and their car. My friend and I jumped in our car and locked the doors, watching in amazement as the two men abruptly drove off the lot. We blinked and the men in robes had vanished."

Gordy's Story

"I work as a custodian at an inner-city Christian school, a job I have been blessed to have for years. The children and their joy and laughter make it all worthwhile; they even have a 'Mr. Gordy Day' every year where everyone wears a funny T-shirt like the ones I like to wear.

"I live not too far from the school, and my neighbors also know they can count on me for help with fixing things. One day, I was up in the branches of a neighbor's tree, trying to help him trim a huge dead limb before it fell off and hurt someone. The crotch of the tree was about twenty feet off the ground, and the branch was about twenty-five feet off the ground.

"There was a rope between my neighbor and me (he was standing on the ground). I told him to pull west, but he pulled north, which made me lose my footing and I began to fall.

"As I was falling, I saw a post down below and I knew I had to avoid it or else be impaled by it. I twisted to avoid the post, and landed on a cement riser between the sidewalk and the grass. My pelvis made full contact with the riser, and I knew it was busted. I got up and hobbled two steps before I collapsed.

"As I lay on the ground, in horrible pain, my primary thought was sadness, because I knew I wouldn't be able to work for a while and I love being around those kids. Then I saw an African-American woman around forty years of age cross the street and come toward me. 'I'm going to pray for you,' she said, kneeling beside me and laying her hands on me. She prayed a very simple, short prayer for peace and healing in my body, and then she was gone. I had never seen her before, and I knew almost everyone in the neighborhood.

"Later on, after rehabilitation in the hospital and at home, I asked around the community and no one knew who this woman might be. I wanted to thank her so badly. What really convinced me she was an angel was the way my older body healed. My doctor kept asking me if I had lingering pain, and I kept telling him no, not really. He finally told me that almost everyone who had this type of pelvic ring injury experienced chronic pain afterward, and he couldn't believe I was fine. I truly believe that this woman was one of God's angels, ministering to me as I lay broken in pieces on the sidewalk. This experience taught me you have to be open to God's work, because it's all around us."

A Brush of Angels' Wings

Janet's angel delivered a message from God. "Otis" and the African-American woman cared for God's children in their moments of need. And angels on rescue missions delivered Missy and Zackary from terrible harm or even death.

My two angels cared for me at a most critical hour, comforting me with their gentleness and strength.

This bears repeating: they didn't have wings, even though they flew me to heaven. Still, winged beings do play a part in this story, as I'll explain in a little bit.

In the Bible, some angels, especially the cherubim and seraphim, are represented as winged in several passages, including Exodus 25:20: "The cherubim shall stretch forth their wings on high, covering the mercy seat with their wings, and their faces shall look one to another; toward the mercy seat shall the faces of the cherubim be" (KJV).

These verses in Isaiah talk about both the throne I saw in heaven and the winged angels:

In the year that King Uzziah died, I saw the Lord seated on a throne, high and exalted, and the train of his robe filled the temple. Above him were seraphs, each with six wings: With two wings they covered their faces, with two they covered their feet, and with two they were flying. (Isa. 6:1–2 NASB)

Cherubim, I learned, not only have four faces (one of each: a man, an ox, a lion, and a griffin), they also have four conjoined wings covered with eyes. After the fall, they guarded the way back to the Garden of Eden and the Tree of Life. They also attend the throne of God. St. Thomas Aquinas had a theory that Satan was a fallen cherub.

Seraphim also serve as caretakers to God's throne as they continuously shout praises to him. I find it fascinating that their name, *seraphim*, means "the burning ones."

Was it the cherubim or seraphim whose wings brushed against my arms and face and head as I stood at the gate of heaven? I couldn't see the creatures that brushed against me, but they felt like the flutter of wings against my skin. To be more specific, the feathers felt soft yet sturdy, like that of a large bird, a Canada goose, a swan, or yes, a stork. The feeling wasn't that of a fluffy, downy baby chick at all.

Peggy's angel story was also told to me after my heaven trip, and when I heard it, I was instantly reminded of how those angels' wings had felt brushing against me.

The Touch of Angels' Wings

Peggy, a Canadian mother of five children, was the kind of mom who always prayed for her kids before they walked out the door to school each morning. One day, Peggy was praying for her two little girls as they were about to leave for school. Immediately after she finished praying for them and opened the door to let them out, she felt a rush of wings graze her head gently. It felt as if a large bird had flown past her, out the door behind the girls. But as Peggy spun around to see what it was, she saw nothing behind her. Still, whatever it was had flown *out* of the house and not into the house. She looked out to the sidewalk where her daughters were walking toward school and saw nothing. No large birds were anywhere to be seen. Suddenly, she knew in her heart of hearts that what she had felt was an angel, following her children and watching them every step of their way.

Isn't that a wonderful, heartening story of God's watch-care for his little ones?

Angelos

I am leaning toward my two heavenly visitors being the most "ordinary" order of angels, simply *angelos*, or messengers. They are the angels most concerned with the affairs of people on earth, and fulfill lots of jobs and undertake all kinds of missions, including flying me to heaven on that incredible night.

As I said, my flight was as smooth as could be, a gliding sensation I'll never forget, because it was like no other flight I ever took on earth. We flew upward at first, for a few seconds or maybe a full minute. Then, I noticed two things: my angels all at once changed course slightly, veering to the right a little bit, before beginning our descent.

Yes, it was a descent, definitely a distinct drop and no longer a climb.

I'm absolutely sure of it. We were gliding downward on an angle when I realized something else. I looked down and saw that my dangling legs had pants on, and that somewhere midair, between this world and the next, my clothes had changed. When my angels picked me up, I had been wearing my blue hospital gown. In the air, I saw that I was now wearing a light brown golf shirt, tan pants, and shoes, the kind of thing I might wear to take my wife out for dinner.

Later, when I would get a glimpse of my precious mother, grandparents, son-in-law, and friends, I would notice that they too were dressed very similarly to what they wore as they lived their lives on this earth.

There's something else I want to tell you about the way I was set down in heaven. Ruth and I are fortunate enough to live in a condo with a bunch of older folks like us as neighbors. I like to relax from time to time in a deck chair by the man-made lake right below our sliding doors, watching the migratory birds that flock to the banks of the lake.

If I've watched one, I've watched a thousand Canada geese come in for a landing by the lake, their brownish-gray wings alight as they coast smoothly toward solid ground.

When I "came ashore" to heaven's gate, I felt like one of those Canada geese, gently gliding toward the ground.

As soon as my feet touched down, my two angels disappeared and I never saw them again.

I had landed in another realm, in the very kingdom of heaven, where I was to see and hear and feel things beyond my wildest imagination. Already, in those sacred seconds in the cloudless sky, I was enjoying myself very much.

3

Lights, Colors,
and a Love Story

The colors and lights in heaven were simply sublime. Of course they were. Would you expect anything less?

They were the deepest, richest, most gloriously lush colors I had ever seen, and some I had never seen before. Heaven is a dream-come-true for those who love all things colorful, and our home there is lit by the Father of Lights, who dropped the sun and moon into the sky. Like the apostle John said in his Revelation of heaven: "The city does not need the sun or the moon to shine on it, for *the glory of God gives it light, and the Lamb is its lamp*" (Rev. 21:23).

The lights I saw were far beyond descriptions such as "radiant" and "luminous," soft and delicate shimmers that were somehow robust, and bold and vigorous beams that were somehow gentle to my eyes.

I simply don't think those colors and lights exist on earth. *Now Marvin*, you may be thinking, *that doesn't help me out in the least. Can you be a little more descriptive?*

Well, I'll give it my best shot. I know "indescribable" is a frustrating word, but I promise you, it fits the situation. But I will try to relate to you the colors I saw in heaven.

I did not see streets of gold. Mind you, I didn't get very far, only to the gate and then a brief peek inside the gate. I like to tell people it's as if you were from Nepal or Congo or someplace, and you were dropped via helicopter into Estes Park, Colorado, and picked up by the same helicopter twenty minutes later. Your impression would be that America was one big mountain range with jagged, snowy peaks because that's what you happened to see during your limited time there.

Other heavenly travelers have seen different sights than I had, and credible witnesses to heaven *have* seen golden streets and people with wings (not angels). Colton Burpo, the precious little boy whose story is told in *Heaven Is for Real*, even saw a magnificent rainbow horse. They are not making up their journeys any more than I am making up mine; we simply were given our own short previews based on what God wanted us each to see.

I did see some phenomenal things, though. The colors and lights were just two of those sights.

The Greenest Green and Bluest Blue

I saw babies and children and grown-ups of all ages playing and talking and laughing on grass that was the greenest green I've ever seen. I'm a golf nut, and I love to settle in each year and watch the crème de la crème golf event, the Masters Tournament, held in Augusta, Georgia. I've only been able to see the grass on which the world's greatest golfers play on high definition TV, but that flawless, emerald-colored carpet is the greenest surface I have ever seen in my lifetime. An acquaintance was privileged enough to attend the Masters Tournament, and his wife teased him because he came home with all these snapshots of the grass. "Check out this turf," he had told her, all excited as she rolled her eyes just a little bit. "See how perfect it is, how incredibly green." Picture the verdant, luscious grass at the Masters and then try to imagine grass far greener and more deluxe. That's how green the grass is in heaven.

The sky in which I flew to heaven, and the firmament surrounding the heavens, were a wilder and bluer yonder than you would ever believe. The atmosphere was soaked in color and light, and the blue was again outside of any tint we can brag about down here.

The closest shade I can associate this otherworldly blue with is the surreal tones of the water in the Caribbean or off the coast of Hawaii at sunset. It's a blue to marvel at, to appreciate and admire wholeheartedly. Imagine the ocean or a tropical bay at its bluest, and then think about the fact that a blue far from that color is waiting for you and me on the other side. And if blue is your favorite color, you're in luck. From what I saw, blue is the second-most prevalent shade in heaven. (Can you take a stab at what the first was? Stay tuned.)

The thing about the colors in heaven is that they are all shot through with a brightness, a luster that seems to incorporate the sun's rays, the moon's beams, a fire's flicker, and a star's glitter, stirred together by a master lighting director and splashed out over the canopy we will spend eternity watching.

How this Master loves to add glow and warmth to our dim paths with previews of the brightness to come!

The Light of My Life

It was 1956, a leap year, the year I took a leap of faith and love that would improve my life beyond measure since that blessed day in June when I laid eyes on Ruth, the light of my life.

Elvis Presley had just hit it big on the radio with "Hound Dog," Rodgers and Hammerstein came out with *The King and I* at the movies, and General Electric introduced a nifty new gadget called "The Snooz-Alarm," the first alarm clock that allowed you to whack it over and over again before you finally came to.

I was twenty-one years old, just out of Calvin College in Grand Rapids, where I had graduated with a degree in economics and business. It was a summer of endless possibilities, as I was courting the girls, sometimes properly and sometimes with all the charm of a nervous wreck. Girls confused me and confounded me; being the oldest of three boys, I really couldn't begin to fathom their mysterious ways.

That summer day, when I was set up on a blind date with a nursing student named Ruth, I wasn't expecting my world to flip on end. I just thought we would enjoy some gooey pizza at Fricano's pizzeria, and maybe I would get the chance to flirt a little with a pretty girl.

I thought she was beautiful. (I still do.) I can't remember how the pizza was that night, but I will never forget those shining blue eyes and her quiet maturity. She was, I thought, one of the most interesting women I had ever talked to. I still think so, after all these years.

However, the draft board was sending me ominous notices. Ruth says I took a month to call her, and I think it was more like two months. It wasn't that I lacked interest, but I was immature and didn't know where my life was headed. Still, a month or two later, I called her, and that was that. There was no one else for me but Ruth from that day on.

So, off I went to basic training with her loving words. In my mind, I knew it was the first time a woman had offered me words like that so sincerely.

We wrote letters back and forth, and those letters lit up my days in basic training. She was a young nurse, just getting started, and her job entailed so much serious business, matters of life and death. Ruth poured out her heart to me in those letters, and I tried to do the same with mine. Once you put it on paper, you can't take it back. I'm so glad we committed to paper our feelings for one another, and got to know each other so thoroughly as the mail flew back and forth from Grand Rapids to Colorado Springs, where I was stationed.

When I came home on leave, we spent every spare minute together. Ruth moved in with my parents to save money, and one day soon after I returned to Colorado, my dad took Ruth to the jewelry store to pick out her engagement ring.

On her next visit to Colorado, she was faced with a miserable sight: her strapping Army beau, feebly lying in a hospital bed, with red, puffy eyes and a hacking cough. At least I was clutching a diamond ring—I had that much going for me.

I was so sick with pneumonia I couldn't even get out of bed to get down on one knee to pop the question. It popped in spite of this, and she took pity on me and said yes. She said yes! At that moment, sick as I was, I felt my soul fill up with brightness.

Dance of the Spirits

Heaven exhilarated me with its greens and blues, but the number one color there seemed to be white. White! I'm not talking about the famous tunnel with the white light. I never saw a tunnel like that, although others have seen it, so I'm keeping an open mind.

White is one of my favorite colors—white and red. We've never owned a vehicle that wasn't white or red.

The white in heaven was—forgive me!—like none other I can compare. From a brilliant white to an opal stone to a milk glass moon color, the white shades clustered in the sky like a huge bridal bouquet, white on white on white, yet all distinct tinges and tones, including some whites God is saving for us to see in Glory. The multitude of whites included brighter whites and lighter whites—they were all gorgeous.

There are three reference points on earth to which I can compare the variations of color and shades in heaven. The most down-to-earth example is the sugary swirl of cotton candy you might enjoy at the circus or the state fair. As cotton candy has lots of different colors spun into it, the colors in heaven would meld from whites into blues and reds and purples and greens. The multiple colors would change and shift and move constantly, twirling and twisting and floating.

The many lustrous varieties of white were, like every heavenly color, infused with glowing light. Now we "see through a glass darkly," and we screw a lightbulb into the wall so we can see to read newsprint and iron our clothes and pay the bills. The lights in heaven are not bolted to any wall. They are constantly moving and shape-shifting in a way that fixated and enthralled me. The closest I can come to describing what that light show was like is probably the aurora borealis, or the northern lights.

About ten years ago, Ruth and I flew to Anchorage, where we rented a motor home and rambled around the great state of Alaska for a couple of weeks. More than once, our Midwestern mouths hung open as we gawked at the spectacle and pageantry of the northern lights.

The Cree Indians call these lights the "Dance of the Spirits," as they two-step around the polar skies, leaping and twirling in patterns of reds, greens, purples, blues, and pinks. And what place is more filled with spirits—real spirits—than heaven?

There the lit-up colors come together, pull apart, do-si-do . . . they jump and spin and twist and spiral and pulsate, kind of like a dance, sort of like the northern lights.

Then again, if I compare the light show in Alaska to the light show in heaven . . . it's not even close.

The Answer Is No

Ruth said yes to the first question and no to the second.

We were weeks away from getting married when I got orders to ship to Germany for two years. Well, that threw a wrench into things. A fellow finds the perfect girl to marry and then the Army comes along and everything gets stalled. I knew Ruth wouldn't be happy about this piece of news. The date was set, Ruth had sewn her dress, and the cake was ordered. She and my mother had already stuffed a couple hundred engraved invitations, licked the envelopes shut, and crammed them in the mailbox. I didn't know much about women, but I did know this news was going to go over about as well as the Hindenburg. Still, what are two years when a man and a woman are in love?

Nervously, I dialed Ruth's phone number on a payphone at the base in Colorado. "Will you wait for me for two years," I gave my halting delivery, "until I get back from Germany?"

"No," she responded curtly. I literally dropped the phone, I was so shocked.

No? Well, that wasn't the answer I was hoping for. As it turned out, though, Ruth was saying no to the two-year-wait, not to me. The Army, in a flash of kindness, permitted me to return home to be married just before being shipped to Germany. I had recently been promoted to company clerk after fifteen weeks of infantryman training.

We telephoned every single person invited to the wedding and told them it had been moved up. On July 9, 1957, Ruth became my wife and has been with me every step of the way, through thick and thin, richer and poorer, in sickness and in health—and literally, through heaven and earth.

The honeymoon was brief and fumbling, the blunders concealed behind a façade of hopeful yearning.

Then, quicker than you can say "gesundheit," we were packed and off to Germany. We were young and full of promise for what was to come. I was married to someone in whom I saw mountains to climb, valleys to explore, and new wonders beckoning off in the distance.

And together, over half a century, we have climbed mountains, more than I can count, but first we had to stumble over a couple of molehills. I am almost embarrassed to tell

Marv and Ruth, family dinner, 1998

you what sent me into tantrums regarding Ruth's behavior within the first month. You see, I suddenly discovered to my horror that this beautiful creature to whom I was married had a horrendous habit: she squeezed the toothpaste tube in the middle rather than carefully rolling it from the bottom!

She also had a new mother-in-law who spoiled her three boys beyond belief. So it was news to me when I found out Ruth wasn't about to iron my undershirts and undershorts like my mother always had. "I'm sorry," she said, in a tone which indicated she wasn't very sorry at all. "But I just don't do that." Well then, that was that. It was either iron my own shorts or wear them wrinkled.

We settled into our new lives in Heidelberg and found some new friends at a little church on the base. Soon after we arrived, I was promoted to chief clerk for the US Army in Europe, which meant I was in charge of 30,000 soldiers' whereabouts. One of these soldiers, by the way, was one Pvt. Elvis Aaron Presley, who was also stationed in Germany during my time there. Were these men and women on field or off? On sick leave? Our biggest concern at the time was Russia dropping the A-bomb, and I took my responsibilities very seriously.

Obviously, I took myself way too seriously as well, if I was going to roll up my guns and shoot over the matter of improper toothpaste squeezing (and ironing undershorts).

Our biggest newlywed fight was about picnicking on the Sabbath. Now, these days I will picnic with the best of them on a Sunday, but back then, coming fresh from the house of the very Dutch and very staunchly Reformed Marjorie Besteman, I had some issues with it. My bride simply could not understand what was wrong with laying a blanket on some green grass and partaking of deviled eggs and lemonade on the Lord's Day. Didn't the Lord himself make green grass and deviled eggs and lemonade for our pleasure? Actually, what she said was, "That's the stupidest thing I ever heard."

After some "negotiating," I came around to her way of thinking on matters of Sabbath observance, and I realized that if anyone was going to iron my undershorts, it would have to be me. And toothpaste? I just gave up and started squeezing the tube in the middle, right along with my beloved.

So as you can see, it was a big job Ruth took on when she walked down the aisle to take my hand and hear the preacher say, "Dearly beloved, we are assembled here to join this man and this woman in holy wedlock." It wasn't long after that she discovered she had a lot of work to do.

Ah, but I do love the fire in her eyes when she's about to vent the air about something. Life is partly for fun, and part of the fun is working out the problems, handling the differences, and struggling for a meeting of the minds. Sparks can really fly when a red-blooded American man and woman in love face off over something that matters to them. You could even call these sparks fireworks—flashy, bold, and colorful, with lots of zing and tang.

Fireworks in the Firmament

One of my favorite holidays is the Fourth of July, when the burgers are sizzling on the grill, the red, white, and blue flags are waving six deep at the Byron Center (Michigan) parade, and the fireworks are exploding in the black sky.

I've already told you the lights in heaven were most like the aurora borealis, but fireworks are another reference point I can use.

Pyrotechnics boomed and crackled (except they didn't make you want to plug your ears like they do down here), decorating heaven in shapes like cakes, spiders, peonies, and of course shapes and formations not of this world.

Every color you can think of—purples, reds, blues, silvers, greens, whites—interwove with each other in shining sequences. I was rooted to the spot in line at the gate, but if I would turn my eyes for a second, I would look up and see another arrangement.

Anyone who thinks they are going to be bored in heaven, plopped down on a marshmallow cloud in a pastel world of harps and floating babies, is dead wrong, if you'll pardon the pun.

Even just the light show was utterly transfixing.

At times, a gigantic color-ball, in constant yet steady motion, with shades slowly weaving in and out, burst above me, kind of like fireworks, sort of like the Fourth of July.

Then again, if I compare the fireworks in Michigan to the fireworks in heaven . . . it's not even close.

A Jar of Fireflies for the Journey

Ruth and I eventually figured out how to sort what really mattered from what didn't matter at all, such as toothpaste tubes and who irons what.

Fatherhood came quickly for me, and my children and grandchildren became lights of my life.

While we were still in Heidelberg, Ruth became pregnant with our first child, Julie. Our German hosts cried their eyes out when we told them we had to return to the US. They had become as attached to us as we to them, despite the language barrier. We loved our time there, but in those days a tour of duty was two years, and our tour happened to be up. We packed our bags again and headed back for the USA.

The first time I held my baby girl, Julie, in my arms, I was busting my buttons with love and pride. She seemed light enough to float away. Somehow, I managed not to drop her. God blessed us with another daughter, Amy, five years later, and then a son, Mark, five years after that.

I've enjoyed every moment I've spent with my children, watching as they grew and watching their minds and bodies expand. I remember hours spent with them when they were small. I remember the sweaty taste of their cheeks when I kissed them. First days at school, their earliest artworks, the way they played the flute and the trumpet and the cornett—all these many episodes brightened my eyes and my life. All of the years I have spent loving my children, I would not alter in the slightest. The joys all of them have provided will never fade. They lifted my spirits during some dark and trying days.

One of the darkest times in my life was when our baby son, William John, died after just ten hours of life. I will tell you more about William and all the babies I saw in heaven later on in my story. For now, I'll just say that anyone who has lost a child knows that our hearts were broken in a million pieces when William died.

Ruth and I learned to handle adversity the same way anyone learns: by going through it. We both determined that the hard things would be used as sealers rather than dividers of our union. Why life is so dark sometimes we do not know, but we do know this: what happens is not as important as what we do with what happens.

As a husband and a father, I've had a lot to learn about marriage, parenthood, love, and what matters most. So much time and distance has come between that moment and this one. We've had times of great joy and deep sadness, but always Ruth has been my beacon, illuminating the passages both dark and bright with her love and wisdom.

In Ruth, God the Father handed me a jar of fireflies for the camping trip of my life. "Here you go, son," I picture him saying, passing me the beaming jar. "It's going to get dark and scary at times. I will be here always, lighting your path, but here's a little extra light for you, just because I love you."

Today after fifty-five years of marriage, I am more sensitive to the thrill of her presence than I have ever been. When I come on her unexpectedly in a crowd, it is like a glad little song rising up somewhere inside me. When I catch her eye in public, it is as though she is hanging out a sign with the exact words of inspiration I need right then. When I drive home in the evening, I must consciously guard the foot pedal, lest I step on the gas too fast approaching the house where she waits for me. I still count the day's biggest thrill when she comes hurrying from wherever she is to greet me at the door with a kiss. Are these the musings of a sappy old man? you might ask. Guilty as charged.

As I look down the road ahead, I see an elderly man and woman going into the sunset hand in hand. I know in my heart the end will be better by far than the beginning.

Basking Forever

After my trip to heaven, Ruth asked me if I had ever thought about her during my time there. Had I ever once thought of our children, our grandchildren? Just like Ruth, she didn't pose the question defensively or with insecurity. She asked out of pure curiosity.

And the answer is, no, I didn't think of my beloveds, as much as I adore them. In fact, had Peter, via God, given me the choice to go back to Ruth, Julie, Amy, and Mark, on earth, or stay in heaven, there's no doubt I would have chosen to stay in heaven.

I would have chosen to stay in that wondrous place of dancing lights and color-bursting fireworks, enjoying every shimmer and beam and texture and tone.

Of course, it's not just the lights and colors that are worth staying for.

It's HIM. He's the sun, the moon, the stars—everything. One day the Son will return and we will be better, finer people. Nothing shall separate us from each other and him.

Together, Ruth and I and those we love will bask in his glorious light forever.

4

At Heaven's Gate

I had been dropped off by angels at heaven's gate. If you picture yourself in my shoes, being nervous or being afraid, don't worry! Your experience will be the exact opposite. I felt fearless and full of wonder. I experienced no nervousness, even though I had been dropped, literally, into another kingdom. If anything, I was totally serene and calm, more peaceful and at ease than I had ever been on my most relaxed day on earth.

Immediately, I saw an enormous door, several stories tall, attached to the gate, and a wall that wrapped around the kingdom in either direction, with no end in sight. It was the biggest door I had ever seen, not to mention the biggest wall and the biggest gate, and so forth.

The wood grain of the doorway was darker than an oak or an ash. If I could compare it to any wood on earth, I would say it was most like a rich mahogany. A plain design was carved on it, nothing fancy, but beautiful just the same, the way simply carved wood can be. Brilliant lights bounced and danced all over the length and width of the doorway. Would I consider it to be pearly? If I had a dollar for every time someone asked me that, I'd buy myself a new golf club.

Well, no, actually, the gate wasn't pearly, but save that thought and we'll explore it later.

There was no top to the door, at least none that I could see. It seemed to ascend twenty or thirty feet upward into a cloud of mist and then vanish.

How did I know it was a door and not a wall? Another good question. For one thing, I found that many times I just knew things in heaven without being told, and I'm sure everyone else who has ever gone to that place feels the same way. There was no tour guide, pointing out the highlights and hot spots or offering trivia about the sights and sounds. There was no angel parked in the front, with a big "Ask Me" button pinned to his robes like we were at some kind of banker's convention in the sky. You just know what you know when you're there, and I knew this was a doorway.

Besides, a section of this massive doorway had a handle, an old wooden handle like something you'd find on a covered wagon. It was sturdy looking, about two and a half feet long and six inches wide.

Heavenly Travelers

There were probably thirty-five people ahead of me in one big line (it wasn't as if there were angels or heavenly gatekeepers, calling, "I'm open on line five!"—the gate wasn't some version of the DMV). I knew without being told that I was in heaven, and so did everyone else. You just knew where you were. No one was asking their neighbor, "Where am I? Am I lost?"

You could tell by the looks on their faces they knew where they were. Everyone was smiling. No one looked shocked or even awed. They all had a look of deep, thorough contentment. Maybe that's why no one said anything to anyone else. We were all in a reverie of peace, joy, and perfect happiness.

The smiles on everyone's faces seemed to say, "We made it! We finally, finally made it!" We were home at last, and we all knew it.

Now, Byron Center, Michigan, is as about as homogenous as any town can be, unfortunately. I say unfortunately because I enjoy the richness of a diverse culture. I love to travel and learn about other countries, peoples, and their foods and traditions. In Byron Center, everyone is the same shade of pale. I am one of countless Dutch men of a certain age and maturity. To be honest, you can't throw a golf ball around here without hitting a Dutch senior citizen in the head.

Heaven was so different. Even the short line of about three dozen folks was a melting pot of colors, cultures, and costumes. I was wearing my normal "uniform," a golf shirt and khaki pants, the exact kind of outfit I would wear in my everyday life. The smiling people who stood in that line were from all over the world and wore all kinds of different clothing. I saw many different nationalities represented, including Scandinavian, Asian, African, and Middle Eastern. How did I know those people were Scandinavian? (I knew you'd ask.) They looked purely Northern European to me, with classic Scandinavian cheekbones and jawlines. But to be honest, that was one of those things I just knew.

A couple of the people I saw appeared to hail from primitive African tribes; they were wearing loose, flowing tribal gowns and toga-like garb with sandals on their feet.

The man in front of me in line was Middle Eastern look-ing. Several years later, on a trip to Turkey, my feeling that my fellow traveler to heaven's gate was from that area of the world was confirmed. This man was in his early sixties or maybe his late fifties. He wore a baggy, brown-colored caftan that looked like he had been sleeping in the dirt. Maybe he was a shepherd, or a subsistence farmer of some kind; he was definitely dressed like an ancient peasant, not a modern Middle Eastern person on the streets of Istanbul. His pants were slouchy and loose too, and he wore some kind of a headpiece or hat on his head.

Most of the people in line were around my age or older, which is the way things should be. Believe it or not, some were even much older than me. Most of the men in line were between fifty and seventy years of age, and most of the women were between seventy and ninety years of age.

There were three children in line, each of them around four or five years of age. These little ones were not standing still, but moving around, wiggling in their spots in line, like children do. They all had big smiles on their faces.

It's terribly sad, I know, to think about children dying, and of course these precious kids had died or they wouldn't have been in that line. Their loved ones were experiencing the heartrending loss of a child—perhaps the worst and deepest loss anyone can ever experience. I wish I didn't know how awful that is, but I do. So what I'm about to tell you is said from a heart that has felt the wretched loss of a child. I don't share this piece lightly. But I promise you, dear one, those children were delighted to be in that place. Their eyes were shining with life and pleasure, just like everyone else waiting for their turn through the huge doorway.

The Mystery of the Indian Baby

Very soon I would see many, many babies in heaven, just beyond the gate, but while I was in line I noticed just one baby. He was of Indian heritage, and was as tiny as a baby would be on his first day of life.

This baby, or rather the people surrounding him, was and continues to be somewhat of a mystery to me. You see, a man who appeared to be around fifty years old was holding the baby, but I got the impression he wasn't the baby's father. Actually, I felt a strong intuition that he was carrying the tiny boy for another person in line, a young woman standing in front of him. All three of them were Indian, but besides that, they seemed to know one another. The young woman, a beautiful girl of about twenty-five or so, was standing very close to the man and the baby, and every time I glanced at her, she was turned around, standing backward in line, and holding intense eye contact with the baby, as if she didn't want to tear her eyes away from him for one second.

The mystery is twofold. As I said, I didn't get the feeling at all that the man was the baby's father. He didn't look fatherly at all; in fact, he didn't appear to be comfortable holding the baby. In some cultures, men rarely hold babies, even their own, but beyond that, I just felt instinctively he wasn't related to the baby, or at least he wasn't the baby's father.

For one thing, the man was holding the little one gingerly instead of tenderly, as if he was afraid to drop it. So who was this man in relation to the baby and the young woman, who I felt sure was his mother? It seemed that the three of them had died together, but I suppose it's possible

77

they died separately. Others who have heard my story have had theories, that maybe the man was the girl's father and the baby's grandfather. Or maybe the man was their cab driver, and they had all died in the same accident. I just don't know. But I did feel as if the girl had just given birth to the baby.

The second part of the mystery was why this young lady had needed someone else to hold her baby for her. One's frailties, illnesses, and vulnerabilities end the split second one's feet touch down on the holy ground of heaven, so even if she was recovering from a difficult labor, she would have been strong and healthy the moment she died. Yet I felt in my spirit that she had just given birth and was unable for whatever reason to hold her baby.

I know for sure I had a renewed body there. I felt so good. I was in terrible pain when I lay in my hospital bed in Ann Arbor: I was as weak and uncomfortable as I ever want to be. In line at the gate, I felt no weakness. Actually, I felt like a teenager again, vital, very awake and alert, strong and as healthy as a horse. Marv Besteman was restored, completely. I was better than ever, truth be told, better than when I was a strong, young buck, playing hockey for a short time for the University of Michigan.

Seriously, it was incredible, how fantastic I felt! When God tells us he's going to renew and revive our bodies, he means it. Even later on, when I saw so many people worshiping God beyond the gate, I didn't see anybody there with crutches, damaged bodies, missing arms or legs. I didn't see anyone who had Down syndrome, or any kind of special needs whatsoever. When you get there, you're going to feel like a million bucks!

This truth makes the fact of the young lady needing someone else to hold her baby hard to understand. Still, God knows exactly what was going on in that line and the circumstances of each beloved child of his, waiting for their turn through that immense doorway. He knows, and he'll let me know when I go back next time.

At any rate, I was pretty preoccupied by my surroundings as I stood in line. Besides the music being sung and played (which was the most purely lovely sound I had ever heard in my life), there was the greatest laser light show I had ever seen in my life going on in the great bowl of blue above me.

The magnitude of the sky and my surroundings! I couldn't take it all in. The colors were sumptuous and profoundly beautiful, and the lights? They were like 10,000 silent fireworks, all going off at the same time. There was so much movement and variety to the lights—I was in a state of wonder, from the time I set foot in heaven to the time I entered the doorway with Peter.

As you can imagine, I wasn't paying close attention to the people in line. Most of the time, I was looking around, trying to take in the marvelous sights of this amazing place.

When I checked back in to look at the people ahead of me, I realized the young Indian woman who had been staring so intently at the baby was at the front of the line, waiting her turn to go in. The three of them had been about four or five people ahead of me. The man who had been holding her baby stood behind her, and I noticed with surprise then that the baby was gone. He had evidently gone in first. How did he get in? I don't know—I wasn't looking! Logically, I would suppose the older man handed the baby to Peter, but I don't really know what happened.

And then again, I had a feeling, confirmed later on when I saw so many babies beyond the gate, that no one had to hold the baby; he could have floated in all by himself. Yes, really. What was it Dorothy said to her dog in *The Wizard of Oz*? "Toto, I've a feeling we're not in Kansas anymore." I and the other thirty-five people in line were in a different world, and the rules of gravity and what people were supposed to be able to do at a certain age just flew out the window, right around the time we lost traction with God's green earth. The baby's mother was next to go in the doorway, followed by the older man.

The line moved quickly. But even if it hadn't, people weren't rolling their eyes and tapping their watches impatiently, saying, "Let's get a move on. My tee time's in twenty minutes." Like me, the others were captivated with every detail of their new world, totally engaged, fascinated, and at ease.

The durations of time between when the giant door opened and closed varied, but the people ahead of me didn't take long. It took thirty seconds to one minute between when one person went in the door and it opened again to receive another newcomer. (I took the most time with the gatekeeper, by far, because I was a special case. But I'll tell you more about that conversation a bit later.) As I made my way through the line, the gate got closer and closer. Soon, I would be first in line to enter heaven.

The Pearly Gates?

The gates of heaven have captivated people's imaginations since the early church, when believers read about John's vision on scrolls, ancient to us but new to them. Through the centuries, the gates have served as the subject of countless discussions, and later on, books, movies, songs, and even jokes. Again, it amazes me how many folks, even believers, wonder whether they'll get past the "pearly gates" and gain admission into heaven. What do the gates look like? Who is the gatekeeper? Is it Peter? And who is allowed through those majestic doors?

I can only report on what I saw, and whom I saw while I was there. As always, the best place to find the answers is in the Bible.

John wrote about the gates after experiencing a vision of heaven while he was imprisoned on Patmos, a Greek island. Bible scholars tell us he had this vision around AD 96, over half a century after his best friend and Savior was crucified and rose from the dead. The written record of his supernatural tour, along with fifteen other visions, makes up the thrilling book of Revelation. Isn't it interesting that this last book of Scripture leaves us with a preview of our future home? We were made for heaven, and John's vision, or "revelation," gives us all a mental picture on which to hang our hopes.

The first details we have of the gates of heaven are spoken in John's own words, and are found near the end of the book at Revelation 21:10–14:

He took me away in the Spirit to an enormous, high mountain and showed me Holy Jerusalem descending out of Heaven from God, resplendent in the bright glory of God.

The City shimmered like a precious gem, light-filled, pulsing light. She had a wall majestic and high with twelve gates. At each gate stood an Angel, and on the gates were inscribed the names of the Twelve Tribes of the sons of Israel: three gates on the east, three gates on the north, three gates on the south, three gates on the west. (Message)

I believe I was at one of these gates, one of three in one wall of a four-sided, cube-shaped fortification surrounding that beaming city called the heavenly Jerusalem.

John saw four walls and twelve gates, but I have no idea which one I was at, or which direction we were facing. If "my" gate was inscribed with the name of Dan, Reuben, Levi, or one of the other tribes, I didn't recognize the markings as such.

Plus, this passage says each gate will be attended by an angel, and I saw Peter, not an angel.

And the gates I saw were not pearly. That's right—not pearly!

Now, where does that belief come from, that heaven's gate is "pearly"? Is it just some kind of folktale or story, passed down through the ages? Actually, the Bible offers real evidence for that concept, found in Revelation 21:21, in which the gates are actual huge pearls that cover the twelve entrances to the city: "And the twelve gates were twelve pearls; each one of the gates was a single pearl" (NASB).

As I tell you my story, there will be a few times where I just can't explain what I saw. This is one of those times. Other heavenly travelers have seen pieces of the gate that they have described as pearly; I believe them. I also believe I was given a different vision, an image of heaven that included a gate made of heavy, dark wood and covered in twinkling lights. I'm at peace with that, and I hope you will be too. Rather than try to be as smart as God, we should just quit while we're ahead.

A final note on this matter: my trusted spiritual advisors have prayed with me and for me as I've come to terms with my time in heaven, and they have suggested that perhaps the gates will indeed be enormous pearls when the New Heaven and the New Earth come to be, in God's timing and plan. After all, I was given a hint of the Intermediate Heaven, the place believers go now when they die. It's a different place from the New Heaven and New Earth we will inhabit after Christ's return. That's a very important distinction to make, so please take note.

My spiritual advisors could be right, or maybe it's another answer altogether. Pearly or not, I'm so grateful I had the chance to stand in the shadow of that marvelous gate!

Was Anyone Turned Away?

When I share my heaven experience with people, I always get the same question: "Did you see anyone turned away at the gate? Did anyone ever come back out the same way they went in?" And the answer is no. No one ever came back once they were inside the doorway.

Why is this question such a burning issue for people? I think many folks, even believers, struggle with feeling 100 percent secure in where they will spend the afterlife. They suffer from uncertainty, and secretly wonder, *Is it possible that I might be turned away?* They wonder too about their loved ones who have gone before them. Maybe those loved ones were not vocal in their faith or were not living their lives according to God's will for them before they died.

People I have spoken to wonder if maybe they can work harder to get into heaven. I always say, accept Christ first, that's the key. Folks always seem to want to put the cart before the horse.

You would be amazed at the questions I have been asked, and the fears people harbor, deep in their hearts.

In my mind, every person there was meant to be there. By the time I got to the door, there were fifty or sixty people behind me. We were, all of us, God's children, followers of his Son, destined for the kingdom of heaven. Everyone in front of me was quickly admitted to the presence of God, his Son, the angels, their loved ones, and all of the saints gathered there together.

I was at the top of the line, next to go inside that door of doors. And then abruptly the door swung open, and I was face-to-face with my best-loved person from the Bible, apart from Jesus, the apostle Peter.

5

Hello, Marv, My Name Is Peter

W hen the man opened the door, he stuck out his hand, eyes lit up in friendly welcome. "Hello, Marv, my name is Peter. Welcome to heaven."

The man who stood before me, holding the door of heaven open, was the apostle Peter himself, the "rock" on which Christ built his church, and Jesus's dear friend.

I must admit—I gaped at him. How could I not? He had always been someone I admired and related to in the Bible, and here he was thrusting out a hand for me to shake.

Maybe I was too distracted by all the sights and sounds while I was in line at the gate, but I didn't put together who he was before he introduced himself.

That's when the lightning bolt hit me. *Peter!* I thought, *Oh my goodness! It just doesn't get any better than this.* (Actually, it did get better, because that's heaven. Just when you think you've never been happier, somehow you have another experience that tops the one before.)

Peter had a strong, confident handshake, and the look in his eyes was warm and open. Even though he was one of Jesus's twelve disciples, and one of history's most famous and admired men, Peter was as humble and down-to-earth as the guy who mows your lawn, cuts your hair, or catches your fish. He really did seem just like a fisherman, with a scrubby beard, shaggy hair, and clothes that looked like he had been wearing them for 1,000 years of hauling in nets and gutting fish.

He wore a fabric belt knotted around his waist, and his robes were dark and grayish, made of a heavier material than the gauzy white fabric the angels' robes were made from. Not one bit fancy or "heavenly."

It was fascinating to me how Peter's clothes seemed to be real work clothes, genuine fishing garb, durable and warm, made for the cool winds on the sea. It's always colder on the water, and his robes seemed designed for that.

He wore sandals.

Peter stood about five feet ten inches tall, solid and husky, with broad shoulders and narrow hips. He was built like a wrestler, or maybe a bodybuilder who doesn't take lifting weights too seriously but nonetheless is quite bulked up. I got the feeling if you were to find yourself in a conflict with him, Peter would stand there like a rock and fight you head-on. He had the manner of one determined; I knew that this guy, as a fisherman, would fish his heart out even if the waves were ten feet high.

He had a rounder face, and his dark hair was straight, not curly or wavy, mostly gray, and hung down to his neck, but it wasn't too long (spoken like a clean-cut banker). *Here's another typical older guy who needs a haircut*, I thought.

Peter seemed to me to be about fifty-five years old, give or take a few years. His eyes were grayish with a blue tint—that surprised me a bit, since most Jewish men have brown eyes—and his nose fit his face, which is to say it was a pretty good-sized, strong, normal nose. Peter had a really nice smile, and thankfully, he was smiling at me.

Peter seemed pleased and happy to see me, and his manner was warm, personable, confident, and friendly, all the traits I looked for when I used to hire people—or not hire them, as the case could sometimes be.

When I ran a bank, I would interview people for the top positions, and I would look for people I could trust right off the bat. Peter spoke in a way that made you believe what he was saying was true.

When conducting interviews, I could talk to someone for five minutes, and there would be something off about the tone of their voice or the fidgety look in their eyes, their shifty mannerisms, and I wouldn't hire them, even if they paid me.

Over countless interviews, I was always looking for people who were confident and decisive, but not too aggressive, kind but not a pushover. We had all kinds of customers at the bank, including those who never smiled a day in their lives and would make your day miserable if they could. My job was often to find employees who could serve those kinds of customers. Peter would have been one of those guys I would have hired. I kept a lot of secrets over the years as a banker, and I could tell Peter would have made a trustworthy secret-keeper.

Wow—the one and only Peter, standing in front of me! Peter, the Rock, a friend, disciple, apostle, sinner, and saint. He was more than an inspiring figure in Scripture; to me, he was like a friend I knew well. Maybe a role model or mentor would be an even better description. Peter was just like me in some good ways and not-so-good ways. And now it seemed like we two determined, decisive men (not to mention two stubborn mules) could actually be real, face-to-face friends.

He stood a couple of feet away, a comfortable distance to have a conversation with someone. We made a little bit of small talk—don't ask me about what. Maybe I was too excited about meeting my Bible hero, but I honestly can't recall what we chatted about those first few moments. I am pretty sure it wasn't about the weather.

"I've got to tell you, Peter. You were always one of my favorites in the Bible," I said.

"Why is that?" he asked, curious and smiling slightly.

"Because you messed up about as many times as I did in my life," I answered.

Peter got a big, wide smile on his face and nodded his head, as if to say, *Uh huh, I know that's true!* The apostle and I understood one another perfectly.

Peter did blow it a bunch of times. He was a hothead, and he sometimes got his priorities messed up. At times, his judgment was flawed, just like the rest of us.

But he was a good, strong follower of Christ, someone who dropped his fishing nets to take up a life of risk and danger for his Master's sake.

This shaggy guy standing before me, wearing fishing clothes and nodding with an understanding gleam in his eyes—Peter helped change the world!

Who Was Peter?

I had always been intrigued by Peter's life as I knew it from the Bible, but after meeting him face-to-face, my interest in him got a lot stronger. Who was this gatekeeper to the kingdom of heaven? What was his life like?

The scruffy fisherman met Jesus through his brother Andrew. The two brothers came from the fishing village of Bethsaida, which means "place of nets" or "fishery." (That would be like me coming from a town called "Lots of Banks.") Day in and day out, they lugged their nets into old boats and tossed them out, hoping for a good haul of tilapia, the money catch of the Sea of Galilee. Today, tilapia is even nicknamed "St. Peter's Fish."

The brothers, who came, not surprisingly, from a fishing family, were living in Capernaum, a lakeside town at the northern end of Galilee, when Jesus called them to let their fishing nets fall and become his disciples, fishers of men.

The first thing Andrew did after meeting Jesus was run to find his brother, so Peter could meet this Messiah too.

And the first thing his Savior did was give Simon a new name: "Jesus looked at him and said, 'You are Simon son of John. You will be called Cephas' (which, when translated, is Peter)" (John 1:40–42).

Peter, of course, means "rock."

After they met and Jesus gave him his new name, Peter rarely left his Messiah's side, traveling with him in his ministry and quickly becoming the leader and spokesman of the twelve disciples (of whom seven were fishermen).

Obviously, Peter was a grown man when Jesus chose him to be one of his closest disciples, which means he was probably born around the end of the first century BC.

He was also a married man, according to Mark 1:30, the account of Jesus healing Peter's mother-in-law.

I wonder . . . before Jesus healed Peter's mother-in-law later on, what did Peter's wife think about her husband suddenly quitting his job, and the only means of income they likely had known, and following some renegade prophet? I wish I had been a fly on the wall the day Peter came home and made that announcement!

We know he lacked any formal education, as did John, also one of the "inner three" group closest to Jesus. Acts 4:13 says this: "When they saw the courage of Peter and John and realized that they were *unschooled, ordinary men*, they were astonished and they took note that these men had been with Jesus."

Peter was a blue-collar guy in a blue-collar place: Palestine, the area considered by educated Jewish folks to belong to *Am harez*, or "the people of the land." This term is not as nice as it sounds. In their day, the term was used in a belittling way to describe those who were ignorant of the niceties and deeper values of Judaism and the Jewish way of life.

When Peter became a man, his home turf was very poor and terribly tense because it was occupied by the Romans. Can you imagine our country being occupied by anyone? It's hard to even wrap my mind around it. I bet you anything the people in Palestine were fed up with Rome, and they were looking for a way out from under that heavy oppression.

And then came Jesus, who saved Peter in a way he never expected and didn't always understand. He watched Jesus turn water into wine, transform a few fishes and loaves into a meal for a huge crowd, and even walk on water. He witnessed Jesus raising Jairus's daughter and Lazarus from the dead, and was even given a glimpse of his Master in his truest glory, in the transfiguration on Mount Tabor. There Peter saw his dear friend talk to Moses, Israel's greatest teacher, and Elijah, its greatest prophet, though they had been dead for a thousand years or more. There Peter saw Jesus shine as only God can shine:

> Jesus took Peter, James, and John and led them up a high mountain. His appearance changed from the inside out, right before their eyes. His clothes shimmered, glistening white, whiter than any bleach could make them. Elijah, along with Moses, came into view, in deep conversation with Jesus.
>
> Peter interrupted, "Rabbi, this is a great moment! Let's build three memorials—one for you, one for Moses, one for Elijah." He blurted this out without thinking, stunned as they all were by what they were seeing.
>
> Just then a light-radiant cloud enveloped them, and from deep in the cloud, a voice: "This is my Son, marked by my love. Listen to him."
>
> The next minute the disciples were looking around, rubbing their eyes, seeing nothing but Jesus, only Jesus. (Mark 9:2–8 Message)

During my time in heaven, I received a small peek at how God shines, and I know I will never be the same.

Yet, Peter, who witnessed his dear friend's transfiguration, still kind of blew it, interrupting the holiest of moments by blurting out his idea of a memorial! And he managed to make his gravest mistakes *after* seeing all of these wondrous things with his own eyes. The Rock became a stumbling block, more in his own way than anyone else's, an example for the ages of how darn human we all are.

I cringe at the story of how Peter betrayed Jesus, just when he needed him most—it's so hard to read—but I also see my own flawed heart in it:

> All this time, Peter was sitting out in the courtyard. One servant girl came up to him and said, "You were with Jesus the Galilean."
>
> In front of everybody there, he denied it. "I don't know what you're talking about."
>
> As he moved over toward the gate, someone else said to the people there, "This man was with Jesus the Nazarene."
>
> Again he denied it, salting his denial with an oath: "I swear, I never laid eyes on the man."
>
> Shortly after that, some bystanders approached Peter. "You've got to be one of them. Your accent gives you away."
>
> Then he got really nervous and swore. "I don't know the man!"
>
> Just then a rooster crowed. Peter remembered what Jesus had said: "Before the rooster crows, you will deny me three times." He went out and cried and cried and cried. (Matt. 26:69–75 Message)

But Jesus always saw in him the man of rock he would become after this experience of messing up so badly. Kind of like how Jesus saw in me the decent and loving husband and father he knew I could be, even though I wasn't always decent and loving.

In my younger days, I drank too much and didn't take my faith seriously even though I knew better. Peter thought he could do everything, just like I used to think. We all realize at some point we are not as good as we think we are. We disobey. We fail those we love.

I made a lot of mistakes in college, when I really didn't apply myself the way I should have, not to my studies or my growth as a believer. It wasn't until I was married and in the Army that I realized God's way was the right way and my way was the wrong way. And then I began to build my life, step by step, on the rock of my salvation.

Jesus knew Peter felt horrible remorse over disowning him in that courtyard, so after his resurrection, he appeared to him first, before any of the other disciples. Peter, who had failed so badly, became the leader of the newborn church, as Jesus had predicted, and the very first to preach the Gospel. Jesus gave Peter a wonderful gift, entrusting his first followers under Peter's care.

The fisherman spent the rest of his life, after Jesus died and rose again, telling others the Good News. After a lifetime of serving his Lord as a missionary, teacher, and evangelist, brave, stubborn Peter died a cruel death for his faith. Tradition tells us that Peter was crucified upside down in Rome during Emperor Nero's terrible persecution, which began in AD 64, the same persecution Peter warned the early believers about in his first letter. They needed that letter so badly. According to historians, many Christians died heinous deaths, being torn to pieces by dogs, burned alive, or nailed to crosses like Peter.

Peter's message to them was one of comfort and hope, full of encouragement to stand firm in Christ, like he did, to the end. Jesus's faith in him was not misplaced—after all, Peter really proved to be a rock.

A couple of years after my heaven experience, Ruth and I journeyed to some of the Bible lands, including Rome, the place from which Peter wrote his letter of warning and comfort to the first Christians, and the city in which he likely died.

As I stood quietly at St. Peter's tomb, under St. Peter's Basilica in Vatican City, I wondered to myself about the man who greeted me so warmly in heaven. Was that earthy fisherman with the firm handshake really buried here, under this shrine of marble and gold? Many pieces of archaeological evidence suggested he was.

But I knew better. I knew where Peter really was. He was in that beautiful, beautiful place where I met him all too briefly, in the service of his Lord and King, perfectly fulfilled and content forever.

And I bet that whenever Peter got the chance, he hopped in a boat and sailed on the shiny waters of the sea I saw, just beyond the gate.

Wait a minute, old man . . . what sea are you talking about? This is the first we've heard of it.

Hang on there, friend. We'll get to heaven's sea in a minute. But first, let's talk about keys, specifically, who holds the keys to the kingdom of heaven?

Peter, Demystified

Who had the man really been who greeted me at heaven's door, beyond a well-known Bible character, canonized saint, and, oddly enough, the setup to countless jokes? ("A rabbi and a priest die and show up at the pearly gates, where they are met by St. Peter . . .") You know what I'm talking about. We've all heard these jokes and maybe even told them.

Here's a good one, for the sake of example, plus it's funny:

As a young man, Norton was an exceptional golfer. At the age of twenty-six, however, he decided to become a priest, and joined a rather peculiar order. He took the usual vows of poverty and chastity, but his order also required that he quit golf and never play again. This was particularly difficult for Norton, but he agreed and was finally ordained a priest.

One Sunday morning, the Reverend Father Norton woke up and realizing it was an exceptionally beautiful and sunny early spring day, decided he just had to play golf.

So . . . he told the associate pastor that he was feeling sick and convinced him to say Mass for him that day.

As soon as the associate pastor left the room, Father Norton headed out of town to a golf course about forty miles away. This way he knew he wouldn't accidentally meet anyone he knew from his parish.

Setting up on the first tee, he was alone. After all, it was Sunday morning and everyone else was in church!

At about this time, Saint Peter leaned over to the Lord while looking down from the heavens and exclaimed, "You're not going to let him get away with this, are you?"

The Lord sighed, and said, "No, I guess not."

Just then Father Norton hit the ball and it shot straight towards the pin, dropping just short of it, rolled up and fell into the hole. It was a 420-yard hole in one!

St. Peter was astonished. He looked at the Lord and asked, "Why did you let him do that?"

The Lord smiled and replied, "Who is he going to tell?"

Now, there's a joke that hits a nerve with me, a golfer from a faith tradition that can sometimes make a big deal out of what its people do on Sunday!

But seriously, Peter's legacy goes miles beyond the punch lines. How, for example, did he become a fixture in those pearly gate jokes in the first place?

We know that, over the years, a version of "St. Peter" has become a standard character in jokes, cartoons, comedies, dramas, and plays—all kinds of storytelling. This "character" almost always plays upon Peter's role as the "keeper of the keys" of heaven, as told in Matthew 16:13–19:

> When Jesus arrived in the villages of Caesarea Philippi, he asked his disciples, "What are people saying about who the Son of Man is?"
>
> They replied, "Some think he is John the Baptizer, some say Elijah, some Jeremiah or one of the other prophets."
>
> He pressed them, "And how about you? Who do you say I am?"
>
> Simon Peter said, "You're the Christ, the Messiah, the Son of the living God."
>
> Jesus came back, "God bless you, Simon, son of Jonah! You didn't get that answer out of books or from teachers. My Father in heaven, God himself, let you in on this secret of who I really am. And now I'm going to tell you who you are, really are. You are Peter, a rock. This is the rock on which I will put together my church, a church so expansive with energy that not even the gates of hell will be able to keep it out.
>
> "And that's not all. You will have complete and free access to God's kingdom, keys to open any and every door: no more barriers between heaven and earth, earth and heaven." (Message)

That's it—the verse on which all of the stories and folklore about Peter at the gate is based. That's why Peter has come to be depicted as an old, bearded guy who sits at the pearly gates, acting as a sort of hotel front-desk clerk who personally interviews entrants into heaven.

This view of Peter has been perpetuated through history, from Medieval artwork, where Peter is painted as a bald man with a long beard (usually there are keys in the paintings too, dangling from Peter's hands or attached to his belt), to the 2004 movie *Millions*, where St. Peter appears to the main character, a young boy, and refers to himself as the "patron saint of keys, locks, and general security."

I definitely didn't see any keys on Peter, and he sure wasn't bald like I am. He had all his share of hair and then some. He wasn't sitting behind a desk and he didn't toss off a one-liner, although he did seem like a man with a sense of humor.

Some people who have heard my story have been surprised to hear that Peter greeted me, because most Bible scholars agree that Jesus wasn't actually referring to Peter as the gatekeeper of heaven. Rather, he was beginning to prepare his beloved disciples for the suffering that would soon come, and reaffirming their authority as his disciples. What Jesus meant, theologians suggest, was that anything done by Peter, or any of the disciples, in accordance with his will would have permanent power and validity, now and forever.

All I can tell you is what I saw and what I experienced, which was encountering Peter himself at the gates of heaven. In some ways, my encounter actually lines up with the theory that Peter acts as the front door man for heaven, or at least for the gate I went to. However, he seemed to me to be more of the designated greeter for that gate and for that day. He certainly wasn't sitting at a desk with a sign on it: "Saint Peter: Admissions Desk. Ring the bell if no one is here."

For sure, it's not up to Peter who gets in and who doesn't, no matter how many jokes and stories suggest it is. I've said it before and I'll say it again: If you make it that far, you're going to make it all the way into heaven. God and only God decides who and where, if and when.

Peter's purpose was to greet me and make me feel welcome, and to check in the Book of Life to see if my name was in there *for that day*. Maybe God chose Peter for this mission—helping me figure out what was going on during my time in heaven—because he knew how much I had always liked him. It's also likely that God knew we were evenly matched in the obstinate department, and Peter could handle this dogged Dutchman, especially when it came time to deliver bad news. Because when he opened the Book of Life for April 27 or 28, 2006, the name Marv Besteman was nowhere to be found.

6

The Book of Life

When I got inside the massive doorway into heaven, there was an area I can best describe as an inner gate. It was like the ones we read about in Scripture, like the ancient gates that still exist in some parts of the world that have been inhabited for many centuries.

As my eyes swept from the left to the right, I saw a long stone shelf that extended about ten to twelve feet in either direction before sort of fading away in a kind of haze or mist. Piled on top of this shelf or table made of stones were books upon books upon books, stacked up three to four books high, all along the surface both left and right.

The stones were rugged and simple. They weren't fancy in any way; rather, they were roughly cut and completely unpolished. It was almost like they fell off the side of a hill and someone said, "Leave them there." I'm quite sure this bench of rocks was, well, rock solid, immovable, able to bear tons of weight. Yet it had a look of loose stones piled one on top of the other, natural and of-the-earth.

In fact, when Ruth and I took a cruise to Turkey, Greece,

and Italy, the kind of gray ash stone we saw all over the Bible lands reminded me of the stones in heaven.

If you've ever been to that beautiful area of the world, you know exactly what I mean. When we traveled there in 2009, I was struck by how rocky and uneven the paths are. When you walk, you have to watch every step—it's so bumpy. On a day trip to Ephesus, the place where Paul sent the book of Ephesians, I stumbled once and fell flat on my face. I thought I had broken my nose.

Not that I'm complaining, because as earthly trips go, this one was wonderful (though we did almost lose Ruth in the Vatican, but that's a story for another day).

On the trip, I kept thinking about the letters delivered to the Romans, the Thessalonians, the Ephesians, etc.—letters written by the apostle Paul, transported by faithful servants, and then read in those very places in which I was walking. Were the letters read aloud to lots of people in coliseums? Or passed from believer to believer? Being in the Bible lands was so inspiring, in more ways than one.

I must confess, I couldn't help but notice Greece had the most beautiful women I had ever seen. Ruth had to hold me back a little bit. I may have been seventy-five, bald, and falling on my face, but I wasn't blind!

Back to heaven and the shelf in that inner sanctum, made of those coarse, jagged stones I saw all over the place in the Bible lands. The shelf was about three feet high, about up to my waist. The books stacked on top of it were about as thick as the Grand Rapids phone book, about two and a half inches. They were bound in what appeared to be ancient black cowhide, worn and antiqued, yet not falling apart at the seams. Like the stones, the books had the patina of ancient days, yet I knew somehow they were stronger and longer-wearing than any books on earth.

It never clicked that these books were the Book of Life, or as I discovered, really, the *Books* of Life, until Peter turned away from me and looked in a specific volume, searching for my name. Then I realized what these books must be, and what their glorious contents were all about.

Peter didn't look through more than one book, nor did he riffle through the pages of the book he opened. He seemed to open it up at the right spot. He knew exactly where to look for my name.

When he opened up the Book, it was as long and wide as an atlas, about ten inches wide by twelve inches long. When Peter turned to look in the Book, he was about three feet away from me. I can't tell you what language the book was written in, whether it was English, Aramaic, or some celestial language only written and read in heaven. I didn't notice that, or the texture of the pages, or how fine the print was, or how small the font.

Why didn't I notice these things? Well, I was a little distracted, let's put it that way. The sights of heaven could hold your attention more than, say, a stunning hockey goal shot from the blue line, or an accident on the highway, or even the lovely ladies of Greece. I had a hard time focusing on the incredible thing happening three feet in front of me—one of Jesus's disciples was looking me up in the Book of Life!—because just beyond that great man and those superb books was a whole new world, the world of heaven itself.

The Greatest and Biggest Roll Call of All Time

Before I saw it with my own two eyes, I thought the Book of Life was like a giant, small-print encyclopedia, like the ones I used to page through as a kid, looking up stuff about constellations and tree frogs and Burma. In my mind, the Book of Life was filled with names, millions and millions of names recorded with care, identifying those who are saved by grace.

I had always been a student of Scripture, studying God's Word for my own spiritual nourishment as well as in my roles over the years as an elder at the churches we attended. But after going to heaven, and seeing some of the things God talks about in his Holy Writ, I wanted to take a closer look at what the Bible says about what I saw, including the Book of Life.

The Book of Life: A Deeper Look

The Book of Life is sacred to Christians as the great registry of those who will be joining the Father, his Son, and his Holy Spirit forever and ever in that perfect place. Christians are not the only ones who consider this book to be holy; it's also a revered teaching in Judaism. In the Jewish faith, the Book of Life is called *Sefer HaChaim* in Hebrew, and is considered to be the book in which God records the name of every person who is destined for heaven.

The New Testament mentions the "book of life" eight times, and seven of those occur in the book of Revelation, in John's vision of heaven. The other reference appears in Philippians 4:1–3, Paul's closing call for faithfulness, loyalty, and unity among the church members in Philippi:

> Therefore, my brothers and sisters, you whom I love and
> long for, my joy and crown, stand firm in the Lord in this

way, dear friends! I plead with Euodia and I plead with Syntyche to be of the same mind in the Lord. Yes, and I ask you, my true companion, help these women since they have contended at my side in the cause of the gospel, along with Clement and the rest of my co-workers, *whose names are in the book of life.*

Apparently, two women in the church, Euodia and Syntyche, were not getting along very well, as happens with everyone from time to time. But Paul refers to them anyway as co-workers in the cause of the gospel, as those who labored alongside him in his ministry, and servants whose names are written in the Book of Life. To me, this classifies the Book of Life as a record of the names of those who have eternal salvation.

Revelation

The other New Testament references to the Book of Life appear in Revelation, specifically in the apostle John's vision of heaven. The first of the seven mentioned appears in a passage about the great white throne judgment:

> Then I saw a great white throne and him who was seated on it. The earth and the heavens fled from his presence, and there was no place for them. And I saw the dead, great and small, standing before the throne, and *books were opened. Another book was opened, which is the book of life.* The dead were judged according to what they had done as recorded in the books. (20:11–12)

Theologians tell us that the great white throne judgment described here is a judgment for unbelievers. Many Bible teachers believe that no one at that specific judgment has his or her name written in the Book of Life. What that means for sure, I don't know. I wish I did.

Only the one who wrote those names in those books really knows. I do know that Scripture is clear that no true believer should doubt his eternal security in Christ.

I love what Jesus says about this in John's Gospel:

> My sheep recognize my voice. I know them, and they follow me. I give them real and eternal life. They are protected from the Destroyer for good. No one can steal them from out of my hand. The Father who put them under my care is so much greater than the Destroyer and Thief. No one could ever get them away from him. I and the Father are one heart and mind. (John 10:28–30 Message)

"No one can steal them from my hand. . . . No one could ever get them away from him." That comforts me deeply, and I hope it comforts you as well. Many believers spend way too much time worrying that they won't go to heaven when they die, that their names are not written in those ageless books I saw.

I wish everyone could have the same kind of preview of heaven I had, that each person saved by grace would feel safe and sure that their names are written in the Books. To me, the Bible is very straightforward on this matter, but not everyone interprets certain verses the same way. Some people point to Revelation 3:5 and their definition of "victorious" as "proof" that a person can lose his or her salvation:

> The one who is victorious will, like them, be dressed in white. I will never blot out the name of that person from

the book of life, but will acknowledge that name before my Father and his angels.

To me, the promise of Revelation 3:5 is obviously that the Lord will never erase a name: "I will never blot out the name of that person." A "victorious" person is not someone who wins every battle against sin; if that were so, the Book of Life would be filled with blank pages. Rather, I firmly believe that this person referred to here is God's precious child, who, through Christ, is ultimately triumphant over the temptations, trials, and evils of this world—in other words, one who is redeemed, safe, written in God's roll call and destined to spend forever with him there.

I like the way *The Message* paraphrases this verse: "Conquerors will march in the victory parade, their names *indelible in the Book of Life*. I'll lead them up and present them by name to my Father and his Angels."

If you love him and have chosen him, you will be one of those conquerors, dressed in white, marching in the victory parade. You will be led by Jesus, his face lit up with a parent's pride and joy, introduced by name to God the Father and his angels. Why? Because your name is indelible in the Book of Life! Yes, indelible—in other words, impossible to remove, etched, permanent, enduring forever.

God keeps good records. He knows his own, and he has set the names of his children for all time in his book.

God's Muster Roll

The Book of Life has been referred to as "God's Muster Roll" by people trying to wrap their minds around this divine volume, framing it in a way that's understandable to our earthly brains. For those of you who don't know what a "muster roll" is, it has a military connotation as an inventory, a roster, or a register of the officers and men and women in a military unit or ship's company. Those searching for their ancestors who fought in the Civil War will be familiar with this idea; they would have to pour over hundreds and hundreds of dusty, brittle pages to find their relative's precious name.

How much more prized is your name and mine, written in the Book of Life! In the Old Testament, this book is also referred to as the roster in which all the people who are considered righteous before God are recorded for eternity.

The prophet Isaiah talks about God's holy remnant, his "branch," a reference to all believers, being logged or classified as holy children of God: "In that day the Branch of the LORD will be beautiful and glorious, and the fruit of the land will be the pride and glory of the survivors in Israel. Those who are left in Zion, who remain in Jerusalem, will be called holy, *all who are recorded* among the living in Jerusalem" (4:2–3).

The prophets Daniel and Malachi also prophesied in the Bible concerning the Book of Life. Daniel 12:1 promises that, in the endtimes, "your people—everyone whose name is found written in the book—will be delivered."

Malachi had a different name for the Book of Life; he called it "the scroll of remembrance." Writing about the remnant again, he wrote, "Then those who feared the LORD talked with each other, and the LORD listened and heard. A scroll of remembrance was written in his presence concerning those who feared the LORD and honored his name" (3:16). Different translations call this the "book of remembrance."

This passage is significant for a reason other than the beautiful imagery of a "scroll of remembrance." It suggests that the Book of Life contains not only the names of those who will spend forever enjoying God's presence in heaven, but also the good things we have done in his name.

Peter didn't mention any of my good deeds, or bad ones, for that matter, when he searched for my name. He also didn't say anything about the tears I had shed in my lifetime, which the Bible says are also recorded in the Book of Life. "You've kept track of my every toss and turn through the sleepless nights," the psalmist writes in Psalm 56:8, "each tear entered in your ledger, each ache written in your book" (Message).

When the Roll Is Called Up Yonder

That day Peter was on a mission to look and see if my name was in the Book of Life, not for a week from then, or a year, or ten years, but for that day. Unlike the musty muster rolls of old-time military operations and wars, these record books weren't yellowed and easily torn. They have lasted eons and will last eons more. From the dawn of time, one of those durable books has had the name Marvin Besteman inscribed in it, for a certain day and time known only to the Record Keeper. For God's reasons, my name wasn't in the Book of Life for that day.

Remember the old hymn "When the Roll Is Called Up Yonder"? It's not sung so much anymore, though it probably should be. The lyrics express my heart so well: "When the saved of the earth shall gather over on the other shore, and the roll is called up yonder, I'll be there."

I took a peek at the "other shore," but it wasn't my time to have my name called. Next time I go, when that grand roll call is announced "up yonder," I'll be there. I'll definitely be there.

7

Inside the Inner Gate
of Heaven

Peter looked in the Book of Life for no more than half a minute to forty seconds at the most. Naturally, it didn't take him long to discover that my name wasn't in that Book, for that day.

As I waited, I had the chance to look around me, in the place I think of as the inner gate, an open-air location between the outer gate and the crystalline passageway that led into heaven.

I stood on green, deluxe grass, the shade of which no earthbound person has ever seen. The space was open and almost empty. Other than the stone shelf I described, the one holding the Book of Life, there was no other furniture, not even a chair for Peter to sit in. Although, when you think about it, Peter probably didn't need a chair. He didn't need to rest even for one minute.

When I looked up, there was no ceiling to the inner gate. In front of me, just a few feet from where Peter was looking at the Book, a glasslike gate rose upward and disappeared into a mist, like the stone shelf did. Behind me, the dark wood gate also vanished in a swirl of filmy vapor.

Peter and the stone shelf were no more than two or three feet away from what I knew instinctively was the gate of heaven. Within moments I would be given a chance to see inside that gate and witness incredible things, but at the moment I was preoccupied with where I stood then and what I saw from there—a shining blue sea.

Lake Heaven

As I said, Peter was wearing the clothes of his day, loose robes tied with a fabric belt of some kind. In my mind, those were fishing clothes, and when I saw the lake or sea ahead, and the fishing boats, I had a sense that Peter could and would enjoy the water whenever he wanted to, though I didn't see a soul out there at the time.

About sixty yards away, in the middle left of the panorama before me, were some old fishing boats pulled up on the shore of a huge, rippling lake. The boats looked worn and aged, not sleek and razzy dazzy like the boats we see zooming around on Lake Michigan. If I saw a boat like the ones I saw in heaven here on earth, I'd think, "There's an old lugger."

There were just a few boats—I didn't count how many—and they lay on a sandy, rocky seashore. The blue of the lake was a darker, less brilliant blue than the shade of heaven's sky, and the surface had a few gentle waves. Like an ocean or one of the Great Lakes, I couldn't see the other side.

I only looked at the lake briefly, because soon Peter was back from checking the Book of Life.

A Hardheaded Hollander

I was in for quite a shock when Peter returned and broke my reverie.

"Marv," he said, looking slightly puzzled. "I can't find your name for today."

"For today." . . . What in the world did that mean? I'm sure my mouth dropped open.

I was instantly disappointed. *What's happening? I thought that once you made it this far, you were in, no turning back?* I was confused, but yet I never once thought that maybe I wasn't really saved.

I knew I was saved. There wasn't the tiniest doubt in my mind.

And Peter had emphasized the words "for today," which meant that I wasn't supposed to go all the way into heaven *that day*. There is, I know, another date God has in mind, known only to him.

Still, I hadn't processed any of this at that point. All I knew was that I did not want to go back in any way, shape, or form. *Nobody who has ever set foot in heaven would want to go back to earth, not even for a second.*

"I don't want to go back," I said. "Can you look again?" Peter obliged, returning to the volume of the Book of Life he had been looking at before. Once again, he couldn't find my name.

The bulldog in me came out as I began to argue with the founder of the worldwide church and one of the New Testament's dominant figures. I might have remembered that Peter did cut off a man's ear one time when he got mad. What can I say? It seemed like a good idea at the time. And I had nothing to lose.

117

"It's taken me all these years, a long time, to get this far, to heaven, and I'm not going back now," I said. "I'm a hardheaded Hollander. It takes me awhile to figure things out. I'm not going back. What can we do?"

Peter didn't say much, but he seemed to know I wasn't going to go back voluntarily—nobody ever would. "I think you're going to have to go back," he said.

He appeared to be thinking the situation through, and finally he spoke: "Okay, the only thing I can do is go talk to God."

I didn't argue with him this time. I actually felt relieved. If my strange circumstance was going to the top, to God himself, then the matter would surely be settled my way, right?

Later, when I was able to do lots of thinking about my heaven experience, I realized something. There are no mistakes in heaven, none whatsoever. Despite all the jokes out there about St. Peter and the gate, no one has ever been accidentally let in and then turned away due to a clerical error! So why couldn't Peter find my name?

I believe now it was all part of God's plan. God certainly wasn't puzzled or surprised by Peter's news that there was a man waiting at the gate whose name wasn't "on the list" for the day. He wanted me to see exactly what I saw, no more and no less. God put Peter in place strategically to be a welcomer and a guide. And there was no mistake whatsoever in what happened next, no slip-up on God's part in what he allowed me to see and experience after Peter left to go talk to him.

Peter turned and walked through the invisible gateway to heaven, and then vanished.

I got as close as I could to the gate, though I couldn't get through. No, I didn't get zapped, but there was some kind of invisible barrier preventing me from pushing through. There were so many things to take in just beyond where I was standing.

While Peter left to go talk to God, I stepped as close as I could to heaven's entranceway. The gate was as clear as glass, though it was a different texture and feel altogether than the glass of, say, sliding patio doors or windows in a home.

I estimate the height of the gate to be about seven feet tall. I'm 6'2", and shrinking fast; the gate was above my head but not so much taller that I couldn't reach my arms up to try to pull on the steel beams. Yes, steel beams, or at least some heavenly version of steel. These beams seemed to be embedded like a huge ribbon in the glassy surface of the gate, fixed within in a giant X shape.

The shape was nearly invisible too, but it had sort of a faint multicolored outline, with red being the most noticeable color. I pressed in close and stared, my eyes popping out of my head. As I looked out into this surreal and beautiful realm, I saw things I will never forget. I saw children and grown-ups of all ages, each one vibrantly healthy, whole, and contented as can be. I saw a multitude of babies, from the tiniest fetus as small as my little finger to bigger babies, toddlers who could jump and play. Was my son William, with his head of dark, thick hair, in this place? I knew he was, and with every fiber of my being I wanted to find him. And then I saw someone I recognized—two people, actually—a couple I had loved on earth and had lost many years before. I pushed and pulled on the gate, but it wouldn't budge.

The touch and feel of the surface was like no surface I had ever touched in my life. I raised my arms and pulled down on the ribbon of "steel." People have asked me if it felt like an iron bar, rounded, like a subway turnstile or a monkey bar. I have to say it didn't feel like that at all; rather, the surface of the ribbon was flat yet elevated, like a raised beam. I pulled down, and nothing happened. I put the full weight of both my arms on the crux of the X and pushed down. Nothing happened.

At some point, I gave up, knowing I couldn't get in. What I saw still brings tears to my eyes, at least once a day. Beyond the gate into heaven were marvelous sights, a vision of the other side, meant to bring wonder and comfort to me, and to you too.

The first marvels God wanted me to witness and tell you about were the multitude of precious babies.

8

Heaven's Cradle Roll

The first thing I saw when I looked out into the huge kingdom before my eyes were all the babies. The doorway had been left open in that middle space, the "inner gate," and I could see through it as if it were glass. You already know I couldn't go through that door, no matter how much I wanted to.

Believe me when I tell you there were millions of babies, from the tiniest unborn baby, about the size of my pinkie finger, to babies who were preterm to babies who were born full term, and every age on up from there.

I felt a physical jolt of shock at the sheer numbers of babies, babies upon babies upon babies, each one cherished and loved. They seemed to be grouped by age, from the earliest stages of development on up. The unborn little ones were all together, and then there was another group of babies who were newborns and very small infants.

Years ago, in many church nurseries, they had what was called a "Cradle Roll." There would be photos of babies born to church members, posted along the wall with the dates these babies were born. It was like a gallery of pride for these new lives growing in the church family. Seeing these babies, grouped by age, it seemed to me like heaven's version of a Cradle Roll.

On earth, there would be no way for the unborn babies to live outside their mothers' bodies, but yet here they were, alive and thriving. I knew these babes would grow and bloom here, perfectly safe, entirely happy, and wholly loved. The second their lives ended, by whatever sad circumstance, on this side, the babies arrived in a world more wonderful than any dreams their parents might have had for them. And if they were unwanted on earth, for any reason, those babies were wanted in heaven, highly valued and beloved.

Somehow, I knew all these things to be true without being told.

Seeing those babies in heaven later reminded me of an unusual museum exhibit we visited once, many years ago. Ruth and I had taken a trip to Toronto with my daughter Julie and her husband, Joe. Julie was pregnant with her first child, our first grandchild, and so we were all riveted by the exhibit about unborn babies being held at a local museum. The exhibit showed how babies develop, stage by stage, week by week.

Julie was completely enthralled, looking carefully until she found the one that would be the same size, in terms of fetal development, as hers was. Her son was being knit together, "fearfully and wonderfully," even at that moment! We all stared in total fascination. No blockbuster movie or playoff game could have held our attention more. We didn't know then if the baby was a boy or a girl. We didn't know then how much joy this child would bring us, or that he would grow up to be a fine young man, handsome, kind, and good, a skilled fighter pilot for the US Navy.

But we knew this: that at three weeks, before Julie knew she was pregnant, Andrew's heart had begun to beat with his own blood, and that at that time his backbone and spinal column had begun to form. At four weeks, he was already ten thousand times larger than the fertilized egg, and at five weeks, his eyes, legs, and hands were taking shape. I saw babies this small in heaven, and their arms and legs were moving. I knew beyond a shadow of a doubt that they were as happy and contented as could be.

Later, it made me think of all the pre-born lives that end on earth, lives that begin again in heaven. No matter how those lives ended, I knew without being told there was breath, hope, and life abundant there, even in the tiniest fetus.

When I thought about heaven's babies afterward, I thought of our other children, our four babies—one lost just after he was born and three others lost to miscarriage. Where were they? What did those babies look like now? If only I could get through the invisible doorway, I knew I could find each one of our lost dear ones.

I say "lost," because of course we lost them. They were gone, to another world beyond our reach. Time after time, when Ruth miscarried, we felt a loss that we would never forget.

Maybe that's why I understand how important it is to share with you how I saw those babies in heaven. I know if you've lost a baby, you can't ever forget that tiny boy or girl.

There was one baby who dominated my heart and thoughts, even in heaven. I never held him in my arms, but I loved him dearly, this small boy with my father's head of thick, dark hair.

Every year on Memorial Day, Ruth and I visit his minia-ture grave in a section of the cemetery called "Babyland." When I think of that sweet bundle now, and the short-but-cherished life he had, I am brought to tears despite the many years it's been since I laid eyes on him.

As I stood there at the gate of heaven, taking in the sight of millions of dear babies, I wanted so intensely to get be-yond that impassable partition to the other side. I knew if I could, I could hold my son in my arms for the very first time.

Baby Questions

When I speak to groups about my heaven experience, pretty much every single time the dominant questions are about the babies:

- What did the babies look like?
- Who was holding them?
- Who was taking care of them?
- Were the babies happy?

And on and on, people want to know every little detail of what I saw in regard to those babies. So many people I've met after my talks are thinking about their own little ones, babies who were miscarried or maybe even aborted.

People tend to open up to an old man with a soft heart; I've heard so many sad stories. It's been my honor to com-fort wounded mothers and fathers like me, who also never got to see their babies grow up.

I try to answer their questions as best I can, and leave the rest of their healing up to God. Seeing those babies in heaven feels like a sacred trust to me, one of the most holy and wondrous pieces of my experience.

The babies I saw in heaven were about thirty yards from me, but I could see them clearly and with quite a bit of detail. If you're wondering how I could see them so well, again, it's because I was in a different world, where the limitations of our sight on earth just don't exist.

I've had glasses for years, before and since my trip to heaven. I can't see a thing without them. But once I landed on the other side, my vision improved immeasurably. My eyesight was way beyond what it had been on earth at the peak of my youth and health. But then again, why should that be a surprise? My eyes, my ears, my brain, my body— everything was performing far above par. It's like I went from a broken down old jalopy to a sleek racecar with a high performance engine, and so did everyone else I saw there. By the way, I never spotted one person in heaven wearing glasses or hearing aids. Hallelujah—I didn't need my hearing aid up there, either!

The Baby Who Caught My Eye

The babies were thirty yards ahead of me, yet it was if I was holding them in my arms and gazing at them—that's how plainly I could see them.

Those precious ones were in all stages of development, from a minuscule fetus several weeks after conception to babies twenty to thirty weeks along in their development.

There were little ones with newly shaped eyelids, noses, and toes. Scientists and doctors tell us that even a seven-week-old fetus can kick and swim, and some of these small

My Journey to Heaven

ones were kicking their legs. We are told that by weeks eleven and twelve, most babies can grab for something with their hands, or even suck their thumbs. I saw babies that small waving their arms and hands, like babies do.

The smallest ones were grouped together. One baby caught my eye, and I knew that he had been aborted—it was one of those times in heaven that I was given a deeper knowledge beyond intuition and impression. This sweet, tiny person was about as big as my finger, and moving slightly. He looked a bit different somehow from the other babies; he was very small yet defined. I can't tell you exactly how old he was, but I would guess between seven and nine weeks. We are told that fetuses that age have every one of their organs in place by then, with miniature bones replacing cartilage, and fingerprints beginning to form. By the eighth week, the baby can begin to hear, and by the ninth week he can hiccup. "Fearfully and wonderfully made," indeed!

I don't know this baby's story, but I knew he was as happy and adored as all the other children in heaven.

Cherished and Nurtured Forever

There seemed to be a continuing graduation of ages and stages. Older babies, those who could walk and talk, were in another group. These older babies had their own special place in heaven, just beyond the littlest ones.

I got the sense the babies were very happy and contented. They seemed completely peaceful and satisfied, lacking in nothing, like a baby who has just had his bottle. I remember feeding my own children and grandchildren,

128

and how they'd be fussy and unsettled before I gave them their bottle. After draining the good stuff to the last drop, they'd just lie there, well fed, cared for, relaxed, without a worry in the world. That's how these babies were in heaven.

One of the top questions folks ask me about the babies is, who was holding them? The answer is, nobody was holding them, because babies in heaven simply don't need to be held. *Well, that doesn't sound very nice,* you may be thinking to yourself. *Those babies were just lying there on the hard ground?*

I might have thought the same thing myself, had I not seen these comfortable tiny ones in heaven with my own eyes. And they really were as comfortable, happy, and ful-filled as any baby I have ever seen on this earth.

None of them wore diapers, although the older babies had some kind of simple clothing on, nothing elaborate. They just didn't have to be fed, burped, changed, or bathed like babies here do.

That's not to say that babies in heaven are never held. I bet they are held and often, because all things are wonder-ful and pleasing in that place, and what's more wonderful and pleasing than holding a baby?

I imagine the grass they were lying close to was softer than any blanket that ever swaddled a baby down here. I say lying "close to" because there was a layer of space between the babies and that green grass. You could al-most say they were resting on air pillows—that's the best way I can describe the surface in which those babies were cradled. They were also cradled in the perfect love of God, wholly joyful and basking in the warmth of his light and presence. Even though there were so many babies, I sensed that the numbers didn't matter. Each one was cherished and nurtured, because there is no more nurturing place we can imagine than God's home. In heaven, there's more than enough love to go around.

William John Besteman

When we lost our little boy in 1960, some people said all the wrong things. They told us it was God's will that he died, or else that there was something wrong with the baby, so that losing him was really for the best.

If you've lost a child, you know these sugarcoated offerings of condolence are about as helpful as a kick in the head. Ruth and I were not comforted by these words. They are the last things we would ever say to someone reeling from the grief of losing a baby.

Right after we had Julie, we lost two babies in a row, within months of each other. Both of them were miscarried very early on, at the six-week mark. Still, they were significant losses.

Ruth had had a totally normal pregnancy with Julie, a textbook-perfect nine months of growing the life inside her. So we were quite unnerved and then overwhelmed by the string of miscarriages and tragedy that followed. When she got pregnant for the third time after Julie, she began spotting almost right away. But we weren't terribly worried, even when the doctor put Ruth on bed rest for the remainder of her pregnancy.

I was working at the bank by then, making peanuts, but that was okay. Back then we were happy to live on love and peanuts (or peanut butter and jelly sandwiches, which was the case). I was at work all day, which left Ruth trapped in her bed, trying to watch a lively toddler and keep her from demolishing the house.

We learned that bed rest doesn't really jive with a busy eighteen-month-old, who loved nothing more than to climb up the cupboards and drink salt—that kind of thing. Soon, relief workers were called in to help, and Julie spent most days with Ruth's mother or mine.

At the thirty-week mark of her pregnancy, Ruth suffered what is called a "placental abruption," a serious complication of later pregnancy; apparently the lining of her placenta had separated from her uterus. She was pale, bleeding, and in lots of pain. Lying in our bed and keeping still was no longer an option, and Ruth needed to be hospitalized immediately. In 1960, this condition also threatened the life of the mother as well as the baby, so we were all worried to pieces. Would I lose Ruth as well as this baby?

Ruth was admitted to the hospital, and she spent the next four weeks on her back, barely moving, a brave warrior mother fighting to save her baby. Still, Ruth is nothing if not resourceful; while lying as flat as a pancake, she managed to knit a sweater for the baby, holding her arms as motionless as possible just above her chest. Later, when she was discharged, a young doctor who had been attending her was surprised to see her walking around. "Ruth, I had no idea you were that tall," he said. The doc had only ever seen her lying there, horizontal. "And I had no idea you were that short," she shot back. Ruth has always been gifted with the one-liner, even in her darkest days.

At thirty-four weeks, Ruth began bleeding heavily, despite her every effort to keep still and the staff's every effort to keep that baby inside of her longer. The doctors had no choice but to perform a C-section and take the baby early. We were told Ruth would have died had they not taken the baby immediately.

Our wonderful doctor, Dr. Grey, had been so good to us throughout the ordeal. (I remember how we paid him $5 a week for a long time, and even that was a hardship. It's funny, the things you keep in your memory, years after a sad event.)

Knowing Ruth was a nurse, Dr. Grey explained the situation to her in medical terms. He was very kind, yet he would not give her any false hope. He told us there was a 10 percent chance the baby would live. Ruth knew this meant the odds were almost impossible. We had very little hope, but the thing about hope is that you grab on to whatever shred of it you possibly can while it still exists.

Our son William John Besteman was born on that day. He weighed two pounds five ounces and had a full head of dark, curly hair. We named him William for Ruth's father and John for my grandfather. (Years later when we had our fourth child, a boy, the last thing we wanted was to name him after me. I am a Marvin Junior, and we had so many mix-ups with people calling our house looking for my dad, and so forth. Our son Mark has thanked us many times that he's not Marvin the Third.)

As Dr. Grey had feared, William had a condition called "hyaline membrane disease," which meant his little lungs were too sticky to expand properly and take in air. Today, they call this infant respiratory distress syndrome, or RDS. In a nutshell, it's a set of symptoms in premature babies caused by lack of a protein that helps keep their airways dry.

This, combined with immature lungs, is what affected our baby. (In 1963, Patrick Bouvier Kennedy, son of President John F. Kennedy and First Lady Jacqueline Kennedy, died of RDS two days after his premature birth at thirty-four weeks, the same number of weeks at which we lost William.)

Today, this disease affects only 1 percent of newborns, yet it's the leading cause of death in preterm babies. Still, had William been born today, undoubtedly the doctors could have saved him, even though he was born six weeks early. Because of the developmental stage at which he was born, and the fact that it was 1960, nothing short of a miracle could have saved our baby.

Ruth never saw her firstborn son. Neither one of us held him in our arms. Back in those days, that was just the way things were done, even though by today's standards it seems cruel. Ruth had lost so much blood she was totally out of it for hours after she had given birth via C-section. She woke up from the surgery a few hours after William was born, but the staff must have felt she was too frail to be wheeled over to the preemie nursery. It was a different time and place back then; the rules were different. As soon as they pulled him out, William was whisked away and placed in an incubator.

I was twenty-six years old; Ruth was twenty-five. I was young and strong and capable, but I felt as beaten down and defeated as a crippled old man that day. I walked down the cold corridor of the hospital in a daze, looking for the preemie nursery where they had taken my son. When I found the right room, I stood rooted to the floor until my feet went numb, and still I kept standing there. A glass window stood between me and my son. Little did I know that many years later another clear divide would separate me and my son, this time in heaven.

Of the ten hours William lived, I must have stood there for six of them, gazing at his tiny little body, swaddled in blankets and lying so still in a glass box. I couldn't hold him, or even touch his arm, smaller than my thumb. I was unable to tell him I loved him, or offer any kind of comfort or reassurance. I was powerless to even stand by his side and tell him, "Daddy's here. Daddy's here." I wasn't allowed any nearer to him than I was, separated by the glass. I felt powerless, and for a father who would do anything for his children, this was a terrible, terrible feeling.

So I did the one thing I could do for him: I stood there and watched over him, staring at him with a mixture of love and agony. Most of the time, I felt numb, because I knew there was little chance he would make it. Tears would roll down my cheeks at different intervals as well; we were losing this baby—it was just a matter of time.

In this miserable fog, I noted that William had his grandfather's full head of dark hair. Our other babies were bald or blonde, but this kid had the Besteman hair in abundance. He lay almost completely still, but every once in a while he would move an arm or a leg. Every time the baby moved at all, it was a big deal.

And then finally he didn't move anymore. When they moved the incubator away from my line of vision, I knew he had passed away.

It didn't take long for me to turn around and make my way to Ruth's room. She had been awake for just a few hours and was still in rough shape from the surgery and losing all the blood. When I walked into her room to tell her our son had died, I didn't have to say a word. She could tell by the look on my face that he was gone.

When I See William Again

People told us afterward, "You can have more children," which is really a knuckleheaded thing to say, if you think about it. Oh, I know, they were trying to be comforting, trying to cheer us up, as if there was a bright side after all. Folks so often don't know what to say when someone loses a loved one, never mind a child. They either say nothing, pretending your loved one never existed, or they blather on with these candy-coated nuggets of "sympathy."

My suggestion in times like these? Say very little, only "I'm so sorry. I love you. I am praying for you." Say little, but show much. Convey your sympathy through hugs, cards, meals, and any practical thing you can do to help.

Because, if you've lost a child, you know that, at that moment, you don't want "more children."

You want the one who has left you, now and always. Oh, you move on, eventually, because that's the way life is. We look at people who lose their first child, and we wonder how they keep going. Our "bright side" was indeed Julie, our busy little girl. We had to keep moving for her sake. But what people don't understand is that your heart never forgets the one you lost, no matter how many more come before or after.

It's a good thing God doesn't put all these things in front of us, for us to know about before they happen.

The worst thing was picking out William's little casket, all by myself. Ruth was in the hospital for at least ten days after the baby died. When I went down to the funeral home, they had these little boxes, all lined up. Oh, it was so very difficult.

The funeral was very small, just me and my parents at the funeral home. Ruth was not allowed to leave the hospital for William's little service.

He has a little headstone, and once a year on Memorial Day we visit the grave and think about what could have been.

We have a nephew, Scott, who would be close to William's age, about fifty-one now. As we've watched Scott grow and as he has reached his various milestones in life, we've thought of William, and what he would have been doing. Would he have played hockey, like me and Mark, or chosen a different hobby? Who would he have married? How many children would he have had?

And then of course we have thought about what he's doing in heaven. What did he look like now? What kind of man did he grow up to be in that perfect place? Or did he grow up? In my mind, he's still my dark-haired baby boy. Others who have shared with me their stories of losing babies long to hold their babies in their arms once they get to heaven. Yet many people believe that babies grow up in heaven. Truly, it's impossible to know on this earth. This is yet another matter best left to God's sovereignty. The most important thing to remember is that all God's children, no matter the age they died, are with him, safe and loved. When the curtain is parted and we can see them again, all will be revealed, perfectly!

Naturally, we didn't have a chance to have William baptized. Now, some people might worry about that, and think that maybe a baby who hasn't been baptized wouldn't make the cut into heaven.

That never bothered me. I never did buy the teaching that you have to be baptized to go to heaven. I knew William was there from the moment the nurses pushed that incubator out of the preemie nursery, and I knew he was in heaven years later, when I was there too.

But once again, I wasn't allowed past the glassy screen to see William.

It was a big disappointment to me that I couldn't get past that gate to find William, but apparently it wasn't the right time for me to find him. Next time I go, God only knows when, I will have a one-way ticket only. That's when all the years of separation will fall away. That's when I'll meet my son, and walk with him and talk with him and be with him until the end of time.

9

The Six People I Saw in Heaven

I grew up on the southwest side of Grand Rapids, Michigan, on Cleveland Street, the oldest of three boys born to hearty Dutch parents who loved us and raised us to love God.

It was all a long, long time ago, but when I think about my childhood and those who raised me up to be the man I am, I feel blessed. Mine wasn't a perfect upbringing, but by and large it was nurturing and secure.

Memories come now in snapshots: we lived close to a pond, and after school on winter afternoons, I would lace up my skates and play hockey with my friends. I'd forget supper. I'd forget homework. I'd forget everything to play hockey. That became my love.

As a family, we would head to Silver Lake on Memorial Day weekend and open up our cottage. What I remember most is my brothers and me shivering in the cold water, trying to get the dock and boat ready. Meanwhile, my dad stood on the dock, giving orders, warm and toasty in his hip waders. Sometimes we'd be in that chilly water for hours. I think my dad thought it would build character.

I was short then. I grew into a tall man, but I was the

smallest kid in my class until the summer between ninth and tenth grade. I must have grown five inches during that summer.

So many years have passed between then and now. I had no idea then of the lasting influence my parents and other family members would have in my life. I had no idea how much I would miss them when they died. We don't know until someone is gone what they mean to us.

Beloved Faces

Beyond the impenetrable gate of heaven was a world I had never imagined, of luscious, green grass and a sky of periwinkle, woven with aqua, knit with cobalt, and laced with sapphire. I know bankers don't usually talk like that, but most bankers haven't seen what I've seen. I've also been told I have a poetic streak.

I had already been captivated by the color and light show as I waited outside heaven's gate. But now, I was actually getting the chance to peek inside. I saw the babies first and watched them for a while.

And then, much to my delight and surprise, I started to see people whom I immediately recognized, just a few of those who had meant the world to me before they died and joined God to dwell in that place he has prepared for us.

There were six of them whose beloved faces I knew. Some of them had been living there for many years, and some had left this earth more recently. One dearly loved family member had died just two months before I saw him. I could hardly believe my eyes when I saw how he appeared, how drastic and complete had been his physical transformation. Oh, how wonderful he looked!

I want you to know what these six people meant to me. I want to tell you how they were significant in my life. But most of all, I want you to think about those *you* love, who live in heaven too. I know how dearly you miss their faces, voices, and touch, because I miss my own heavenly residents the same way. When I tell you about the six people I saw in heaven, and how drastically altered, yet utterly familiar, each one was, I hope you find deep comfort in the telling. I know you want them back with you—it's only human to want that. But I promise you, they are healthy and whole beyond your wildest dreams.

What would you do for the chance to lay eyes for just a few more moments on someone you've loved and lost? What would it mean to you to share eye contact and trade smiles and wave at them and have them wave back at you? You'd probably give anything, especially if you knew that your loved ones have never looked better. No matter what manner of death they faced when they left this earth, I'm telling you—those you lost have never looked more alive!

Some of my loved ones died in old age, frail and diminished, yet having lived many good years. Other lives ended much too young, falling to horrible, debilitating diseases. The way they looked when they died broke the hearts of all who treasured them. But how they appeared when I saw them in heaven? Each one was a miracle.

Grandma and Grandpa Besteman

The first people I saw in heaven were my grandparents, Grace and Adrian Besteman.

They were about twenty yards away from me, inside the gate. I could have thrown a football easily and Grandma or Grandpa could have caught it. I tried again to push my way in so I could run over and say hello and hug them, but the unseen "force field" wouldn't shift one iota.

My grandparents were separated by about ten feet; each walked separately but both of them saw me right away. Grandma smiled and waved, and I waved back, hardly believing my eyes. She had been gone for so many years. Grandpa, my old fishing buddy, grinned at me and motioned for me to come inside. He had been gone even longer than Grandma.

My Besteman grandparents had arrived in America as young people, immigrants from the Netherlands. They met in Grand Rapids and raised their family there. Grandpa was in the produce business, like so many of the Dutch immigrants. He dealt with all kinds of fruits and vegetables, buying them from the markets in Chicago and having them transported to Grand Rapids. I remember there were always cut-up carrots and celery with something to dip them in on their table when I'd come to visit as a boy. Grandma, a petite lady with a knack in the kitchen, had a way with banana bread. I never smell a loaf of banana bread baking without thinking of her.

Grandpa had the patience of Job. When I remember him, it's usually a memory involving the two of us sitting for hours in a boat on Baptist Lake, waiting for a fish to nibble. We'd troll for pike or maybe throw in some lures for bass, but it seemed we always sat and sat, he the uncomplaining grandfather, and I the seven-year-old with ants in my pants.

Four generations
of Bestemans:
Marv, his father,
grandfather, and
great-grandfather

Marv (right) and
his brother, Ron

Grandpa and his
son, my dad, both died
with a full head of curly,
black hair. And here I sit,
bald, without a hope in the
world of getting any of it back.

But baldness was the last thing on my mind as I stared at Grandma and Grandpa. They had both died in their old age, bedridden and withered versions of who they had once been.

Yet, here they stood before me, just sixty feet away, flourishing and vibrant, with rosy cheeks and a spring in their steps. Both of them were wearing clothing similar to what they wore on earth, and they appeared to be the age they were when they died. Still, Grandma and Grandpa looked like no other eighty-five-year-olds I have ever seen walking around here. I kid you not. Had I thrown a pass at them, both of them gave the impression they could've easily jumped up and snatched it, thrown it back to me, and started a rousing game of tackle football. Grandma and Grandpa! I was totally amazed.

Mom

Then I saw my mother, Marjorie Sweers Besteman, the mom who had poured her heart and soul into her three boys. My heart jumped when I saw her—I had dearly missed her—but again I was held back from entering heaven beyond the gate.

She was the best mom a boy could ask for. My parents' place was a favorite spot for my friends to hang out. We lived next door to an empty lot with a basketball hoop, for one. But the main draw was my mother, who fed me and my friends almost continuously. She would take out a batch of cookies and start the next batch before that one had cooled down.

My mother never put away the vacuum cleaner. When she wasn't baking, she was vacuuming. And even though she was a big, strapping Dutch woman, Mom always, always wore a dress. I'm fairly sure she wore some kind of dress/bathing suit hybrid to the beach too.

She was thoroughly dedicated to her three boys, attending all of our ball games in good weather and bad. In some ways, she was a single mom, as my dad worked sixty hours

146

a week or more, six days a week, running the produce distribution company. He bought and sold vegetables and fruits through the J. A. Besteman Company, just like his dad before him.

When I was a teenager, I had a curfew of 11:00 p.m. If I was out too late with the car, I could never get away with it. Dad would leave for work at 1:00 a.m. most nights, and he would feel the hood of the car when he left home to see if it was cool or warm. If it was warm, no car for me for a week. He took the keys away and gave them to my mother for safekeeping. Little did he know Mom would always feel sorry for me and relent after about two days. This is what I mean by us boys being spoiled rotten by the woman.

My mother had a very open mind in some ways, and she had an earthy side to her. She had a saying, "If you put your bottom in this chair, your legs will follow." But she didn't use the word "bottom." Actually, there are a few sayings my mom had that I can't repeat in this book! Ask me sometime and I'll tell you all about it.

Yes, Mom was open-minded, unless one of her boys was being naughty, and that was that. She kept a ruler on a peg over the door to each of our rooms. If we stepped too far out of line, that ruler would come down and she would start whaling on us. Have I mentioned she was a strapping lady? Ouch! But yet, in many ways she let us get away with murder.

Other than us stepping over the line, there was one area in which Marjorie Besteman did not have an open mind: she was a stickler for observing the Sabbath, and that's putting it mildly. In her mind, Sundays were a day for devoted reverence to God, a day set apart for attending church morning and evening, and showing deep piety in the hours in between. At least we had to *show* piety to whoever might be watching us. We boys could dangle our feet in the water off the dock at Silver Lake, but we couldn't immerse our whole bodies in it, no matter how hot it was. We could play ball behind the house where no one could see us, but not out front. And we could ride our bikes in the basement but not outside, where the neighbors might see us and allegedly stumble in their walk with the Lord. If it sounds legalistic to you, imagine how hemmed-in a trio of rambunctious boys felt. But despite this one ironclad rule, Mom was usually a softie to her boys and we loved her dearly.

She adored us boys, but her biggest disappointment in life was that she didn't have a girl. Later in her golden years, she had six granddaughters in a row and she was in her glory.

Mom lived a long, happy life, eventually dying at the age of ninety from heart failure. In her last days, she had lost so much weight she hardly looked like herself. I remember one of the last things she said to me: "I never wanted to be the first one to go. Take care of your dad, Marv. He won't last more than six months after I am gone." Dad actually lived six more years and hadn't yet died when I had my heaven experience. He must have been heartier than Mom thought he was! Incidentally, when my dad died in his nineties, his eyes were terribly clouded, nearly blinded, with macular degeneration. The second before he closed his eyes for the last time, his eyes cleared up completely. God had restored his sight, just in time to see heaven's sights.

The last time I saw Mom, she was fragile and weak, her chubby cheeks sunken and gray. One by one, her organs were shutting down. I wasn't there at the moment her life actually passed on, but when she did, it was such a blow to me. She was old enough to die—even I was old by that time. But you only have one mother.

As I stood there at heaven's gate, feet rooted to holy ground, I was given the gift of seeing this beloved person one more time before I go back for good. She was a little closer than my grandparents, and I could see clearly how she looked and what she wore. Mom looked like she had gained back that fifty pounds she had lost during her illness. She looked robust, with pink, round cheeks and a bounce in her step—just like my old mom, whose whole world was her boys. Other than the fact that there are no vacuum cleaners in heaven, everything was the same. And she was wearing a dress, just like the ones she used to wear around our house on Cleveland Avenue, when she'd bake cookies and vacuum her floors and chase her boys with a ruler or a hug. Mom smiled her beautiful smile at me, her firstborn son. She waved to me and I waved to her. Like my grandparents, she gestured for me, as if to say, "Come here! Come here!" But still, I couldn't get through, no matter how badly I wanted to.

Paul and Norm

At that moment, I caught sight of a good friend of mine, Paul, off in the distance to the left, about a half a mile away. In life, he and I had played many games of tennis together, and he had been a spiritual giant in my life. He was in his middle sixties when he died of acute leukemia. In a bitter twist of irony, Paul died in the same hospital I was a patient in while I was there for my insulinoma. We both went to heaven, but I came back. He's still there. Lucky Paul!

Paul was one of those guys who was just excellent with details. He and I served on many church councils and committees together, and I looked up to him for his tremendous faith. Paul had more trust in God than anyone I knew. He would step out in faith, sometimes without a job, and God would always come through for him.

The last time I saw Paul, he and I both decided to have our cars serviced on the same day at the Cadillac dealership. We sat and talked a long time as we waited for our cars to be worked on. He told me he had had some tests run, as he wasn't feeling real well. Even then, Paul had a suspicion that something was wrong.

He was right. After that chance meeting, Ruth and I drove to Florida for the winter and I never saw him alive again. (Of course, when I saw him in heaven, he was more alive than ever.) Friends reported to us long distance how much he suffered back home in Michigan. Acute onset leukemia is just like it sounds: dire, and sets in fast. Everyone told me that Paul looked terrible before he died. In his prime, Paul was around 6'3", 230–40 pounds, with the kind of belly that sent a clear message: this guy does not like to miss a meal. But if he weighed 140 pounds when he died, he was lucky. He was skinny to the point of being emaciated, like so many cancer patients are in their last days. Once he was admitted to the hospital, he never left. Paul went downhill fast, sleeping all the time and floating in and out of consciousness. I was sad to hear that my old friend had died such a difficult death.

I don't think my eyes could have gotten any wider the entire time I was in heaven, and seeing Paul was just one of many unbelievable sights. He too was hale and hearty—my big, brawny friend was back to his old self, roughly 230 pounds. Those who knew him had one question when they heard I had seen him on the other side: Did Paul still have that Santa Claus belly?

And you know what? He did!

Just seconds after I absorbed the fact that I was seeing Paul with my own two eyes, I spotted another friend, Norm, about six feet away from Paul. (Paul and Norm were friends, yet it didn't seem like they were walking together, at least not at that particular moment.) Norm was also a fine Christian man and devoted church leader. He was also a businessman, like Paul, and I very much appreciated Norm's and Paul's understanding of what it's like being a Christian in the business world.

Norm had been a dedicated golfer and a man who loved to fish. Nothing made Norm smile more than a boat ride on Lake Michigan, casting his fishing rod and reeling in the salmon, one by one.

Both of my friends were prayer warriors, and we had spent many hours praying together. I'm not sure if this is why God chose these two guys for me to see—they were significant to me and my spiritual life.

Everyone I saw had been influential in shaping my life in some way.

Sad to say, Norm had also fallen victim to cancer, and he too died a painful and agonizing death, his weight falling drastically. Those once burly arms that could hoist the biggest salmon out of the lake shriveled down to wasted and bony twigs. He died two months before my trip to heaven.

Now, as I gawked at him and Paul, I could only shake my head in awe. Norm was his same sturdy, strong self. Both of those guys looked as if they had never been sick a day in their lives. Each of them had their full heads of hair back, and they were wearing leisure clothes, the kind of clothes they might have worn on the golf course or out for dinner with their wives.

Both of my friends saw me, and their eyes lit up with recognition, their faces split into grins as they too waved for me to come inside the gate. ("What do you think the people at the gate thought when you didn't come in?" Ruth has asked me from time to time. And the answer is, I don't know. But nobody seemed sad or upset about it, that's for sure. They also didn't seem to realize that I couldn't come in, no matter how much I wanted to. Why? Again, I don't know. Perhaps folks on the other side are blissfully oblivious to everything on our side of heaven. As I knew certain things without being told, I am certain my loved ones also had far wider and deeper knowledge than we have on earth. Yet they didn't appear to know that I couldn't get in, as they all heartily motioned for me to come on in. It's just one more puzzle piece of my experience, to be solved when I go back for good.)

If only I *could've* gotten inside—I so dearly wanted to get closer to my grandparents, my mother, and now Paul and Norm. And I knew if I could get past the gate, I could find William John.

I pushed against the intangible entranceway once again, but it didn't give even an inch.

Why Did I See Those People?

When I talk about who I saw in heaven, people who know me and who have lost loved ones (especially those I knew on earth) are eager to know if I also saw their wife, husband, son, daughter, parents, or friends.

The truth is, there were hundreds of people I *could've* seen—I knew them to be in heaven—whom I just didn't see. This doesn't mean for one second that those I didn't see weren't there. They are there!

This is something I have pondered time and time again— why did I see the six precious faces I did see, and not so many others?

Since my experience, of course, I've read just about everything I can get my hands on written by those who have glimpsed heaven. And one thing seems to be true of them all: they see those who had been influential in their lives. Don Piper, author of *90 Minutes in Heaven*, saw his grandfather, a childhood friend who had died when Don was in his teens and who had been key in leading him to Christ. He saw two teachers, who had also played major roles in his life, and his Native American great-grandmother.

It's never come to me exactly why I saw those particular people and no one else. Oh, I've prayed about it, asked God many times. I've thought about it so many times, and I don't know the answers. Why did I see my Besteman grandparents and not my Sweers grandparents? Why did I see Norm and Paul and not so many other friends who have died? The best answer I've received is simply that God chose them for his reasons, and that's got to be good enough for me. My spiritual advisors have suggested that those people were important to me spiritually, and it's true—they all were in one way or another.

It's endlessly intriguing for me to think about why those six were there to greet me. Who will be there to hail me next time I go (for the second and last time)? Will it be the same six, or others? Think about it a minute. Who do you think will be there to greet you?

At this point, you may be wondering why I called this chapter "The Six People I Saw in Heaven," when any monkey could count the people I've mentioned and arrive at the number five. I haven't told you yet about the best reunion of all. Moments after I spotted Norm and Paul, I saw the one person I longed for the most, the one whose death had cracked this old man's heart in two: I saw Steve.

10

Losing and Finding My Best Friend

My eyes went as far left as they could see, over that great gathering of saints. And then, about fifteen yards away, about the length of your average driveway, I saw a really close friend, my unlikely best friend—my forty-two-year-old son-in-law, Steve.

I pressed hard on the invisible gateway again, harder than I had before, but it just didn't move. All over again, my heart hopped with joy, and my eyes and smile got as big as they would stretch. Steve! He was supremely alive in the midst of this wonder and beauty.

The first time I saw Steve, he was a skinny college boy, a fellow student of my daughter Amy's at Central Michigan University. They were dating, and Amy had brought him home to meet Ruth and me. He didn't seem especially nervous, and I remember thinking that he was as polite a fellow as you'd ever want to meet. Never in a million years did I think this smiley kid would one day become, after Ruth, my closest friend and confidante.

When I got to know Steve, I knew I could trust him with my daughter. He was the type of guy who would be a loyal

Marv and son-in-law Steve (right)

husband and faithful provider, working hard to support his family. When he came to me and asked for Amy's hand in marriage, I said the same thing to him that I had said to Joe, Julie's husband: "Are you sure you can support this young lady in the manner to which she is accustomed?" I was joking (well, half joking). "Can you afford to maintain her?" A man with a daughter is probably only going to get the chance to have his prospective son-in-law over the barrel a couple of times in his whole life, if he's lucky. I figured I should make the most of it and have a little fun with the situation. But of course I said yes. And I've never regretted it for a second.

He Called Me "Dad"

Steve was a great guy. With his servant's heart, he was always so willing to help other people. If you happened to be stuck on the side of the road with a flat tire, Steve would be the guy who would stop and help you fix it. He'd come over on a Saturday and say, "Dad, do you need anything done around here?" And we'd go to the hardware store, get what we needed, and get the job done together. He was a terrifically loyal person, someone you wanted for a friend, because if he was your friend now, he'd be your friend forever.

Steve prized fishing the way Ruth and I prize golfing. He'd go pan fishing all the time and come back with walleye and pike. Luckily, he was generous with his catch; our freezer was full of fish.

One time he gave us a huge hunk of all different kinds of fish just frozen together in a massive block. I thought we'd have to host a fish fry for twenty people to get rid of it all!

Good thing Steve loved to eat. He was the first one at the table and the last one to leave, and he never lost a chance to tell Ruth that she was the best cook in the world (she loved that). We marveled at how much food a skinny guy like that could put away. After he finally finished piling all that food in, he would help clear the table and wash the dishes. Seriously, Steve was as perfect a son-in-law as any man could ask for.

Yet, I was taken aback when he came to me with a question not too long after he and Amy got married. Two or three months after their wedding, Steve's dad had died, far too young.

Members of the Besteman family

He came to me about six months later with the question: "I don't have a dad anymore, and I need one. Will you be my dad?"

I said I would pray about it, and that yes, I would try to be his dad. But he didn't want me to tell anyone, not even Ruth. It was our secret, and that change in our relationship was what bonded us so strongly.

In the years to come, Steve would come to me often and ask me for advice about everything. He had lots of questions about raising their two children—how to mete out punishment and praise, parenting techniques, problem solving, and so forth. I felt I had made mistakes many times while I was raising our kids and had learned from

160

those mistakes, so I gave him the answers I had gathered from trial and error. Steve asked me about spiritual matters, marriage, emotions, relationships of all kinds, and quite a bit about financial issues. He didn't always follow my advice, but he asked and I tried to answer as best I could. We talked and talked and talked. And gradually, over years of heartfelt conversation, we became as close as any father and son could be.

The Prime of His Life

By the time Steve was diagnosed with Ehlers-Danlos syndrome, in 2005, I couldn't imagine life without my bonus son.

I had never heard of Ehlers-Danlos syndrome (also known as EDS), but I sure didn't like the sounds of it. Research statistics show that EDS occurs in one in 5,000 people, and it is known to affect both men and women of all racial and ethnic backgrounds.

I'm no doctor, but Ruth is a nurse and a darn good one. She and I became very familiar fast with this rare condition that had stricken our Steve. Ehlers-Danlos syndrome is a group of connective tissue disorders, characterized by extreme joint mobility, skin that pulls easily off the bone (doctors call this "extensibility"), and delicate, fragile skin tissue. The syndrome is named after two doctors, Edvard Ehlers of Denmark, and Henri-Alexandre Danlos of France, who identified it at the turn of the twentieth century.

Apparently, Steve and all those who suffer from EDS have a flaw in their connective tissue, the tissue that provides

161

support to many body parts such as the skin, muscles, and ligaments. The easily breakable skin and unstable joints found in EDS are the result of faulty collagen. (Collagen is a protein that acts as a "glue" in the body, adding strength and elasticity to connective tissue.) EDS patients don't have this glue, and so they are prone to dislocate bones. Steve was always having sports injuries. He would dislocate a knee, and then a shoulder, and then a finger. We just thought he was very unlucky and susceptible to injuries. No one suspected anything more serious than that.

His veins were just dissolving, we learned. One doctor told Steve and Amy that during an operation, trying to suture a vein affected by EDS was like "sewing spaghetti." Another image we were given was comparing his veins to a tire being blown out. His vessels would just burst, causing internal bleeding.

Super-flexible joints are also a key feature of the disease. People with EDS can often bend their fingers all the way back, or grab a section of their skin and pull it up, creating a bizarre-looking tent, as if that person had lost 100 pounds and now their skin was too loose.

Depending on what kind of EDS you have or how it mutates in your body, the severity of the disease can vary from mild to life-threatening.

A biopsy in February of 2005 confirmed that Steve had the syndrome, and that his case was severe, although we didn't begin to grasp how severe until months afterward. There is no cure, and treatment only helps slow down and manage the symptoms. Steve's doctors monitored his condition closely, telling him to use extra caution when engaging in the slightest activity, or even playing with his kids. Any kind of accidental blow, especially to his midsection, could make his symptoms so much worse (Steve was having aneurisms in his midsection). He couldn't run and jump around and wrestle with the kids like he used to, especially not when a basketball to the belly would have been the worst thing in the world.

He began to tire very easily. Even mowing the grass was so hard on him that he had to come in to lie down for quite a while to recuperate. It took so much out of him.

At one point, around December of 2005, the possibility of surgery to correct the problem was brought up. Spaghetti or not, there was a chance the doctors could operate and possibly fix the blood vessels so they wouldn't be so delicate. People in his life advised him to have the surgery soon. But Steve was firm: "I'm not ruining my kids' Christmas."

Losing Steve

Never once did we think Steve would die from this, although in hindsight I can see that I just did not want to go there in my mind. Amy never asked the doctors if Steve would die; rather, her question was, "What's his life going to be like?"

"Compromised," was their answer, which I took to mean that he would have to sleep a lot more and take extra precautions in his everyday activities. Overall, the doctors had given Steve and Amy quite a bit of confidence that he would live a semi-normal life.

We felt good enough about Steve's prognosis that we left for Arizona for the winter months, as usual. I had no idea when I said goodbye to Steve that I was saying goodbye until our meeting in heaven.

When we got to Sun City, we were in frequent touch with Steve and Amy over phone and email. His surgery was scheduled for the beginning of February, and Ruth flew back to Grand Rapids to take care of the kids while Steve and Amy drove to the Cleveland Clinic in Ohio.

They packed their van and drove the six hours, taking down the seats in the back and making a bed with pillows and a mattress, because the doctor said he would have to lie down the whole trip home. They expected him to come home. I expected the same thing.

Did he know he might die? I think he had a feeling deep down he might. So many people had prayed for him at his church, and when Ruth said goodbye, he was stoic. "Just give me a kiss and we'll be off," he said to her, in a breezy way. I think he was tired of people carrying on like he was on his deathbed already, and wanted the goodbye to be businesslike, not dramatic or drawn out.

His pastor had written him an email in which he asked him if he was ready to die. Steve's answer was yes. But he didn't want to dwell on it, that's for sure.

After his initial surgery at the Cleveland Clinic, Steve suffered a cardiac arrest. Sadly, he never got on top of it again after that cardiac arrest. Three more surgeries followed in the next nine days, and after the second operation, they didn't even bother to close him up again. Things were as grim as they could possibly be.

When I realized that Steve could die, I threw everything in the car and drove from Arizona to Michigan by myself. It's a long trip, and I had many hours to think about what was happening. I prayed and cried and prayed some more.

Back at the hospital, Julie and Mark and Steve's mother and brothers had joined Amy at her husband's bedside, where he hovered between life and death. Steve was on so many pain medications, and he was hallucinating a lot and not making much sense. But he didn't suffer—for that I'm so thankful.

After the fourth surgery, the doctors couldn't stop the internal hemorrhaging, and Steve basically bled to death. That cheerful, skinny kid with the heart of gold was gone— it was impossible to take in.

In the middle of the night, when the phone rang at Amy and Steve's house, Ruth knew it was bad news. Mark was calling to tell her Steve had died. Then I got the dreaded phone call, from Ruth, and . . . well, I'm choked up just remembering it all. I can't even express how I felt. It was the hardest thing I have ever gone through. My daughter had lost her husband and my grandchildren had lost their dad. How those kids would miss their dad! How Amy would miss her husband!

Steve was so talented, and so young—far too young to die. I would have gladly taken his place so he could live into his seventies like I had. His family adored him, and the kids loved him at the school where he taught. I remembered that he was so excited about heading up the robotics club at school and now there would be no one to head it up. You think of the strangest things when someone dies, don't you?

I went over to Amy's house, and together Ruth and I told our grandchildren they had lost their father. There are no words to describe their shock and grief. I myself cried like a baby. I had lost my son-in-law, and I had lost my best friend.

Walking, and Leaping, and Praising God

Two months later, I was to see Steve far sooner than I had ever expected. After my trip to heaven, it took me awhile to tell my family what had happened. At first, I didn't want to tell anyone, not even Ruth. (I'll explain further on in the book why it was so difficult for me to share my experience. But this piece of the story relates to Steve.) When I finally broke down and told Ruth, though, the ice was broken, and not too long afterward I told my three children.

You want to talk about an emotional night? Tell your daughter where her husband is and that he's waiting for her. I'll never forget that evening, the intensity and sorrow of it mixed with joy and awe.

Amy was in deep grief over losing Steve, and she was grappling with a jumble of emotions, like anyone who has grieved a dear one's death. She was very angry and felt so alone. And now her dad was telling her he had seen Steve with his own two eyes in heaven? It was confusing for everyone to know how to feel, especially Amy. She probably wanted to feel as if Steve was one way or another still in tune with her, aware of her struggles on earth. When she heard that Steve was joyful and radiant, blissfully unaware, it seemed, of her mourning and her loneliness, it was not completely great news. In some ways, it made her feel even more detached from him and even more alone.

I tried to be as sensitive as I could. It didn't help matters that I told my kids that all I wanted to do was go back to heaven. "Don't be in such a hurry, Dad," they said, looking worried. From their perspective, it was astonishing news, yes, but also hurtful. Didn't I love them and want to be with them?

Oh yes. Those kids and grandkids are my heartbeat, and I'd move mountains for them if need be. But had they seen and heard what I did in that glorious world, they would understand that no one who sets foot in heaven would ever want to come back.

Steve did not want to come back, of that I'm sure. When I saw him beyond the gate, just fifteen yards away, so close and yet still unreachable, I was thrilled. We made eye contact, and both of us had huge smiles on our faces. He looked as cheerful as could be, as if he had just caught a world-record bass and was on his way to weighing the thing. The sickliness that had settled around him like a gray blanket those last months was gone, and Steve appeared as strong and vigorous as any man would ever want to be. He was jumping up and down, waving to me enthusiastically. Jumping up and down! The guy who had been living half a life that last year, cautious and constrained, not up for so many of the activities and pleasures he had taken part in when he was healthy, was now bouncing like an exuberant child. The chains of this earth—sickness, weakness, and worry—were gone.

What a sight for sore eyes. My dearest friend, valued son-in-law, cherished gift from above, was free. Steve was free!

11

After I Woke Up

I t felt like forever while Peter went to check with God to see if I could stay or had to return. In reality it was probably only a matter of minutes, maybe five to ten, although it's hard to judge exactly. I wasn't wearing a watch, nor would I have checked it had I been wearing one.

I saw such magnificent sights in those minutes—perfect, contented babies, a divinely beautiful lake, sublime colors, the smiling faces of six loved ones, and so much more. Just to state the obvious, these were the most awesome (in the true sense of the word) moments of my entire life.

As far as I was concerned, the most important thing to me was getting through the gate to join my dear ones and meet the God I loved, whose love I could feel so strongly in that place, warming my soul like a fire.

Peter came back at last, slipping through the imperceptible gate with a slight smile on his face. He had a look in his eyes like he might have a secret for me.

"Marv," he said firmly, looking at me with those intense eyes, "I talked to God, and God told me to tell you that you had to go back, that he still had work for you to do on earth. He still has work for you to finish there."

I was about to start arguing again, but it was too late. The decision had been made, and I had no choice in the matter. The next thing I knew, I was back in my hospital bed at the University of Michigan Medical Center, hooked up to a web of tubes.

"I Want to Go Home"

Back in my hospital room, it was like an attack of lights coming on—harsh, glaring lights assaulting me like a bucket of ice water on a hot day. It was infinitely brighter in heaven; after all, it's lit by God himself, yet there my eyes had no trouble adjusting to the brilliance.

I was attached once more to all of those tubes—and the pain! I hadn't realized how blessedly free of pain I had been in heaven. Now the throbbing and the hurting was back, full throttle.

Two nurses came rushing in to check on me. Ruth told me that it wasn't standard procedure for two nurses to come in. Usually, she said, a nurse will be assigned to a patient and check that patient all by himself or herself. As for why they were rushing in like that, I just don't know. Something on my monitor must have alerted them that I was in trouble.

I think I was crying even before they came hurrying in, checking my blood pressure and oxygen levels and the tubes and IV.

Once they realized I didn't need medical attention (at least, not in the way they were worried about), they noticed I was bawling like a baby.

"Why are you crying?" one of the nurses asked me. I

can't remember if she was nice about it or not. Nothing or nobody seemed particularly nice to me at that moment.

"I want to go home!" I wailed.

"You have to go back. He has more for you to do. . . ."

If I could have, I would have stomped my feet like a ticked-off four-year-old. I didn't care one bit if there was in fact "more for me to do." I wanted to be back in that perfect, gorgeous, painless place, not lying there in misery, covered in tubes.

The nurse's answer was kind and well meaning. "It will be awhile before you get to go home, Marv," she said, peering down at me. The lady had no idea I was talking about heaven, and not Byron Center, Michigan.

How could I even begin to explain this to my nurses? Were they believers? I had no idea. I didn't want to take the chance that they weren't. Obviously, the one nurse already thought I was acting like a dotty old man, confused enough to think I could walk out of there a few hours after major surgery. If I told them which home I was really referring to, they would have thought I had totally cracked up. I could just imagine the snickers at the nursing station!

I really don't remember the next day very well. I was still in horrendous pain no matter how often the nurses upped my pain medications, and Ruth says I was shaking all over.

Apparently, I had some visitors, friends from Grand Rapids. I knew for sure these friends were believers, yet something stopped me from telling them too. Who would believe a story like mine? I didn't want my friends to think I had slipped a cog mentally.

And a spark of resentment had begun to burn inside of me. Why did God pick me to have that experience, and then make it so fantastic and incredible I couldn't even tell anyone? Was he trying to play a joke on me, to transport me to that place of endless wonders—and then send me back?

Why me—Marvin Besteman, retired banker? Why not pick someone flashier and more eloquent? I've wondered that a thousand times. (Later, my spiritual advisors said, "Why not you?" And they had a point.)

He has more for you to do. . . .

Probably a thousand times or more, I thought, *I wonder what he has for me to do?* For months after my experience, I wondered over it like a dog worrying a bone.

After spending five days in the hospital, I went home to Byron Center.

When I had entered the hospital to have my surgery, it had been winter. But when we left, it was the very beginning of springtime; the air had warmed, with blue skies and budding trees.

We were eager to be out of the hospital and outside again. Yet there was no comparison to the beauty and comfort of heaven. As we drove west toward our home, I knew beyond any doubt life as I knew it could never be the same.

Letdown

After settling in at home, first on the couch and then slowly up and about in my normal, everyday life, the thought that I would never tell anyone, not even Ruth, kept getting stronger.

I hoped maybe that the experience would somehow pass away, like a glorious dream, and I wouldn't have to tell anyone. I had no desire to discuss it with one single soul.

But the opposite happened. It didn't fade away at all. I couldn't stop thinking about what I had seen in heaven and the people I had seen there. My time there started to become a kind of obsession.

I became quite depressed, struggling daily with the letdown of coming back from heaven to this dark world. Wrestling constantly with what had happened and why it happened made my depression worse. I was lethargic and apathetic about life, and Ruth began to worry about my mental health.

Then one day, without warning, the dam burst. Five months after my trip to heaven, in the last week of September, I finally broke down and told Ruth. I don't know what made me tell her, at long last, but suddenly the story just poured out of me.

She's a terrific listener, my Ruth, and never have I appreciated that quality of hers more than when I was recounting my time in heaven.

I cried. She cried. We would dampen our hankies, and start boo-hoo-ing all over again. It took hours to tell her everything, and then all at once I was done.

"Marv," she said decisively, when she could finally get a word in. "You have been truly blessed."

We decided together the best course of action would be to tell our children and swear them to secrecy. And that would be it. (Can you believe I still thought I could get away without telling people about heaven?)

We told the kids shortly after I had spilled the beans to Ruth. They weren't jumping for joy, and they weren't calling me a liar, either. I would say their reaction was somewhere in the middle.

Like kids do, even middle-aged ones, they said, "So, now what?" They were naturally shocked and maybe in some disbelief at first. They knew I would never make something like this up, but perhaps they thought I had been dreaming or hallucinating. It would take everyone awhile to process this unbelievable news.

With that load off my chest, I went back to thinking I could sit on this episode for the rest of my life until those two angels came back for me and carted me off to heaven, this time for keeps.

The only problem was, this was really a terrible plan; God knew it and deep down, I knew it too. The Lord decided I needed a shove in the right direction, so he gave me a hernia, of all things, and sent me on my way to the doctor. And not just any doctor would do. No, God handpicked the physician who would be more than a healer to my body, he would be a healer to my troubled, stubborn soul.

Two One-in-a-Million Cases

It's almost impossible to pull one over on Ruth when it comes to my health and well-being. So, as much as I might have liked to hide the mysterious bulge in my stomach that appeared one day, she was having none of it.

The bulge was an abdominal hernia, she announced, in her crisp nurse voice. She made an appointment with a gastroenterologist that day and also shared her view that it was quite possible that in light of this hernia we were not going to go to Arizona for the winter after all. That's what

I was afraid of. After forty-plus years with a woman, you can read her mind, and unfortunately, she can read yours.

So I had no option but to go to the gastroenterologist to have my hernia checked out. I chatted with the doctor about this and that—the weather looked like it was going to storm, they were calling for the coldest winter on record, and so on and so forth.

He examined me and agreed with Ruth on two counts: I did have a hernia, and golfing amid palm trees was probably out of the question in my condition.

Oh, I was going to Arizona, alright. "Just try and stop me," I said, stubbornly.

"Oh no, you're not," he replied, cheerfully.

We bantered back and forth, or was it bickering? Have I mentioned I'm hardheaded?

I was sitting on the examining table, dangling my legs while the doctor sat in his swivel chair, pondering my case.

He wanted to know what happened to me in Ann Arbor; apparently he thought maybe there was a connection between my surgery there and the hernia now. I told him I had been operated on to remove a rare pancreatic tumor called an insulinoma. Had he ever heard of it?

The doctor paused a little too long. "I've never had a patient with insulinoma," he said slowly. "But I know someone who had it."

"Well, who could that be?" I said lightly.

"My brother."

Now it was my turn to pause. I was totally amazed. After all, insulinomas are less than one in a million, and here my doctor's brother had also been stricken with one. I was very curious about his brother's case, and started to ask questions when I noticed he had tears welling up in his eyes.

He told me that when they had opened up his brother to perform the surgery, they found advanced cancer, and the doctor's brother had died three months later.

I began tearing up too, out of compassion for my grieving doctor, and also because I had become so emotional after my heaven experience.

Looking back, I can see now that the incredible "coincidence" of me having experienced the same rare illness as his brother had formed an instant bond between me and my doctor. Suddenly, the boundaries of patient and doctor fell away and we were talking intently about personal things, as though we had known each other for many years.

"Are you a Christian?" he asked me, out of the blue.

When I answered in the affirmative (although somehow I think he already knew the answer), he and I delved into a really meaty conversation in regard to Christianity, the church, theology—you name it.

"Two things I'm concerned about most are heaven and hell," he said after a while. "What do you know about hell?"

"Well, I don't know much about hell," I said, "only what the Bible says about it, which isn't too much. I think it's a terrible place, and basically it's life in the absence of Christ."

By now, the doctor had stopped watching the clock entirely. My appointment had by then taken far longer than a normal visit to the doctor ever should take. I wonder what those poor nurses and receptionists told the doctor's other patients, waiting way too long in the reception area.

His next question, though, blew the lid off everything, and practically guaranteed that anyone waiting to see this doctor might have to wait all day: "Tell me, then, what you know about heaven."

Uh-oh. I was in big trouble. What did I know about heaven? I didn't have a clue where to start. I wasn't planning to tell anyone except for my close family members, and here my doctor and new friend had asked me about it, point-blank. What could I possibly say in reply?

Then God made it perfectly plain, obvious enough for even a hardheaded Hollander to understand. "Marv, this is one of the reasons I sent you back," he said to me in an audible voice. Yes, I heard God's voice, out loud. And he wasn't messing around.

His words were spoken like an order, a direct command from him to me.

Well then, there was no turning back from God's voice. I told my doctor everything, start to finish, ending my story about an hour later.

I believe the Holy Spirit had prepared his heart to receive my story—he was so receptive to every word. Some other physicians we've told my story to have brushed it off, but this doc was completely ready to hear about my heavenly trip.

The doctor and I finally emerged from his office, and we walked over to the nurse's desk to schedule my hernia surgery. We both had red eyes, and we had been in his office for an hour and a half. The look in the nurse's eyes seemed to say, "What in the world just happened in there?"

So much had happened, for both of us. I had been searching since April 28 for the reason I was sent back from heaven.

Unexpectedly, through the course of an appointment with my gastroenterologist, I had the answer I was looking for. That conversation, and God's instruction to me, was an important part of why I sit here today, telling you my story.

Sometimes—and Ruth will gladly attest to this—you have to explain something to me once or twice before I get it. God in his graciousness had revealed to me what he wanted me to do: Tell as many people as possible about my time in heaven.

The next time I visited this doctor for a follow-up appointment, he introduced me to one of his nurses. "This is the man who saved my life," he said, not elaborating one little bit.

I smiled at the poor bewildered nurse. "And this is the man who saved my life."

We were both telling the truth. The doctor never really explained what he meant by it, but if I were to guess, I'd say that hearing my story of heaven gave a man who was unsure about the afterlife all the belief and security he was craving.

As for me, the doctor had played a large part in helping me understand why God had sent me back. It was to give people like that dear man a message of hope, to brighten the darkness in their hearts, to help them not fear death so much and instead truly look forward to their future in heaven.

It was like the reset button was pressed on my life on earth, which became more meaningful with each person I told.

After that first doctor's appointment, it was like the dominoes began to fall, and I started telling folks more and more often. Our dearest friends Jack and Ruth heard the story when we got to Arizona that winter. (I got to go after all. See, I told you I was stubborn!) I told them they'd have to get their hankies out, and so of course they thought I was going to die of some incurable disease. As I told them my news, they were relieved, then shocked, and finally dampening those hankies, just like I predicted they would.

I told one brother, and then the other one. It took me three sessions, but I finally got the whole story choked out to my patient pastor in Michigan. At first, it was so hard to talk about, especially the part about seeing Steve in heaven. I still can't talk about that part without having a lump in my throat.

But now I understand Peter's words. Offering folks some peace, security, and comfort, and reminding them that their inner sense of the eternal—"eternity in their hearts"—is true, that this world is not all there is, that's why God sent me back to earth.

I don't know how long I have, I really don't. None of us do. But while I am still here, I want to tell as many people as possible about heaven, and about God and his Son, whom I saw seated on the brilliant white throne, gleaming in the distance.

12

Until We Meet Again

I didn't see the throne right away when Peter went to talk to God about whether I could stay or go.

I saw so many marvelous things through that crystal clear gateway, but yet they were just a hint of "the things God has prepared for those who love him" (1 Cor. 2:9).

As my eyes eagerly swept over that panoramic view of heaven, soaking in the sight of endless wonders, eventually I beheld the throne, where our God and his Son are seated and will reign forever.

The throne was about three quarters of a mile away, and dazzlingly bright, lit with brilliant, white lights. It's hard to imagine as I sit here in this dark earth, remembering, but in heaven my eyes could see much clearer and much farther away than they ever could down here.

I saw huge white pillars surrounding the throne, and an enormous crowd of people, men and women, boys and girls, dancing and singing along in a mass choir of praise to the two Beings seated on it. Yes, I did say the men were dancing, and their arms were raised, too, in worship!

Some of my Dutch, Christian Reformed friends are going to have a hard time imagining themselves dancing in worship, or even raising their hands. All they have ever known in a worship setting is stand up, sit down, turn to page 54 in the hymnal (I mean, the "blue book," which is really a hymnal but for some reason that's not what it's called anymore). No matter how devoutly we love our God, raising one's hands in praise is unthinkable, even for me. One of these days I am going to give everyone at church fits and just raise my hands high—let 'em think what they want to think.

Probably, what they would think is this: "Good old Marv went to heaven—he can't help himself."

Well, nobody is going to be able to help themselves at the foot of God's throne, worshiping the two Beings I saw from a distance, exalting the Holy Ones with a purity and joy we have never known.

Yes, I saw two Beings, indescribable images really, but they appeared to be two people sitting there. I've always assumed those two people were God and his Son, Jesus.

How I would have loved to be closer! To see my heavenly Father and his Son who died for me, face to face—even I can hardly believe what's ahead for us in heaven.

We'll experience life as we were always meant to live it, before the Fall, without stress, pressure, negativity, fear, anxiety, sickness, and death. We'll never worry again about what people think of us, which means we'll do things there we never thought ourselves capable of here. Sorry, guys, you're going to have to dance. And the strange thing is, you won't mind one bit.

Heaven is like that—in God's sinless home you are finally free to truly live and happily serve your Lord in whatever work he has prepared for you.

Before I had my round-trip, I never would have thought myself capable, either, of being a firsthand witness to the mysteries and majesty of heaven. And by no means could I have imagined the mission he had for me, to become his messenger of hope and comfort to others.

Did I Really Die?

After I started telling people about my heaven experience, the question was often brought up if I thought I had actually died or "just" been given a preview. Soon after I told Ruth about everything, we wrote the University of Michigan Medical Center and tried to find out what had really happened that night in 2006. Many people I spoke with about my experience wanted some kind of proof or verification. Ruth and I also wanted some kind of substantiation, she even more than me on account of her being a nurse. ("That's just the way we nurses are," she told me.) So, we sent away for lab reports, X-ray reports, surgical reports—everything that was printed, they sent to us. We weren't too terribly surprised when all of these documents revealed nothing.

The one thing we didn't get from the hospital that we would have liked to have was the nurses' handwritten notes. That might have told us more about what happened, and especially why those two nurses had come rushing into my room as if I was on fire. Yet the next day when Ruth asked about how my first night post-op had been, no one told her anything had been out of the ordinary.

But what happened to me was way out of the ordinary— it was extra, extra-ordinary, and it doesn't bother me that we don't have some kind of piece of paper with the hospital's stamp on it to prove it.

While I don't know exactly what happened to me that night, for reasons known to God alone, I was given a preview of the life ahead. Somewhere between life and death, here and there, I received a peek of what is to come.

I know that God wants me to tell you what I saw and trust him with the details. I won't know until next time I go to heaven whose lives were touched by my experience, but God has let me pick some of that fruit here on earth.

After the dam broke and I started telling my story to anyone who would listen, I began speaking in front of small groups of people at churches, in homes, in hospice centers. Folks often stay behind afterward to tell me things, often stories they've never told anyone before. I've heard confessions of people's own brushes with angels and heaven, and of babies loved and lost, long ago or recently. Sometimes, I even hear about how my story has comforted someone or led them on a different path.

I once spoke in a home setting to about twenty people, all related to one another via the hostess. She invited a bunch of family members, but she only had one person in mind: her nephew, who had drifted away from the church and his faith.

After my talk, the nephew came up to me and told me something remarkable. "I'm going to make sure I see you at the gate someday," he said with tears in his eyes. "I know now I need to get back to a church that tells the truth about Christ."

Once, in a large church, a twelve-year-old girl came up to me after my talk and grabbed my hand and would not let go. She was crying her eyes out. "I need to tell you, I've made a decision to be baptized and join the church," she said. "I want to make sure you are watching for me and waiting for me at the gate."

Children usually have fantastic questions. They are very direct with what they ask, which I appreciate.

"How did the ground in heaven feel under your feet?"

"Did the angels have wings?"

"Who was taking care of the babies?"

So many people want to know about the babies, and so many have stories of babies they are longing to see someday. A woman came up to Ruth and me after one of my talks and told us about her son who had died of SIDS. A parent never forgets, no matter how old they get. Our friend found deep relief in hearing about the healthy and contented babies I saw in heaven. "It's such a comfort to know he's in a happy place," she said.

At the Departure Gate

I do feel an urgency to tell people about my experience, because who knows how long I've got until I go back? That's why I wrote this book, even though I'd rather be golfing. Ruth has to handle the requests to have me come and give my talk; otherwise I'd say yes to everything. She says God has impressed upon her that she shouldn't let me overdo it, so we are listening to him and praying for wisdom at every turn of this unexpected adventure.

Since going to heaven, I can't say I've become Holy Marv, with a halo around my bald head, floating above the ground. If I tried to walk on the water of the man-made

My Journey to Heaven

lake outside my condo door, I would surely get my legs wet and muddy, and I'd look like an idiot to boot. I'm still the same old seventy-something sinner, believe me!

But God does feel so much nearer to both of us, probably because we seek him out for everything, the smallest thing, now. Things that we may have considered too insignificant to pray about in the past, we now pray about. One thing I do talk to God about is giving me the chance to tell my story to whomever he might send my way.

A perfect example: Just yesterday Ruth went golfing all day and left me home to do my thing. Our thermostat started to go haywire, and the air-conditioning started failing. I called the heating and cooling company, and they sent over a young man to fix it. After he had made his repairs, the young man spied a book on my table, written by my coauthor. We chatted about that book, and I said she was also writing a book with me about my trip to heaven. He was totally taken aback, as so many people are. I don't know what he expected, but it wasn't that! We talked about ten or fifteen minutes and he told me he had been raised Catholic but hadn't been to church in years. He and his wife had just had a baby, and they were both talking about returning to church for the baby's sake. The young man seemed to take my story as confirmation that he should turn around and get going down the right path again. He ended up leaving our condo with a smile on his face and a DVD of me telling my story tucked under his arm.

One of the most meaningful parts of my mission—and also the hardest part—is becoming a tour guide of sorts for those who will soon be leaving this earth. "Some glad morning, when this life is o'er, I'll fly away," the old song

Until We Meet Again

goes. These dear ones I am guiding are at the departure gate, waiting for their own smooth and peaceful flight in the bluest of skies.

My good buddy Irv just died, which broke my heart in pieces. I wish you could have known Irv. Once he was stuck to you, you couldn't get rid of him; good thing you didn't want to. He had a way of attracting people to him and was the most loyal friend a man could have. So many people visited him in his last days it became a joke at the hospice where he eventually died of cancer: "Too bad Irv doesn't have more friends." Everyone loved Irv, including me.

It makes me feel really good to know where he is right now, and that I was able to prepare him somewhat for the journey ahead of him. Before he died, I spent hours at his bedside, telling him every detail I could remember about heaven. Irv even got to read some of this book before he died.

We have a contract: the first one to go to heaven will meet the other one at the gate. Irv and I talked about this pact many times.

When Ruth and I walked in the door of Irv's church for his funeral, we spotted his wife, who is also our dear friend. When we greeted her, the first words out of her mouth were these: "He's waiting for you."

A Choir of Angels and Saints

Every day since I got back from heaven, I have heard some of that divinely beautiful music I heard in God's home. Mostly, I hear from one minute to six minutes of this music in the middle of the night, but sometimes I have heard

191

pieces of it in broad daylight, while I'm golfing, driving, or reading.

From the second I touched down on the holy ground by the gate, I was surrounded by the most gorgeous music I had ever heard. A million stellar voices (there are no cuts in this choir!), a thousand organs, a thousand pianos—it enveloped me like pure grace.

In John's revelation of heaven, he heard the same glory-filled sounds: "Then I looked and heard the voice of many angels, numbering thousands upon thousands, and ten thousand times ten thousand. They encircled the throne and the living creatures and the elders" (Rev. 5:11).

Most of us don't sing too well on this side of life, but in heaven, there are no off-key or tone-deaf singers. If you've always wanted to sing like an angel, but you can't carry a tune in a pail, just wait and see how fantastic your vocals will be over there!

Every note of this music praised and glorified God; I heard so many "alleluias" from the singers.

The songs I heard were mostly familiar to me, songs that had inhabited my praises on earth for so long.

"Jesus, Jesus, there's something about that name . . ."

"The King is coming, oh, the King is coming . . ."

"Praise the Name of Jesus."

"Holy, Holy, Holy."

"What a Friend We Have in Jesus."

A pastor once asked me a great question in regard to the music. "What about someone from a primitive tribe in, say, Africa, who has never heard choir music?" he said. "Would he hear something different, something more familiar and beautiful to him?"

That's a great question, isn't it? I always hate to specu-
late, though people always want me to, but in this case, I
will offer a guess. I happen to think it's very possible that
you will hear the music you enjoy. If heaven is going to be
pure bliss, why not assume the God who created music in
all its forms will offer something for everyone?

It's also possible the music could have changed the second I left heaven, just as Peter could have spoken another
language to the next person he met in line at the gate.

Whatever our musical styles, I have no doubt we will all
love the music in heaven.

When I hear heaven's music down here, it's always my
very favorite songs from what I heard there; there's never
anything "played" that I don't absolutely adore. This is
music I could listen to forever and ever—and someday, I
can!

I'll Wait for You

Listen, Jesus tells us, "I am the way and the truth and the
life" (John 14:6). Everyone who believes that is welcome
in heaven.

I want you to know about the reality of Christ and the
realness of heaven. I want you to know that total peace
and joy await you. Are you getting excited?

If you have felt unloved in your life, and we all have
from time to time, please know that you will feel so utterly,
wholly loved in heaven. Why, there was nothing unloving
there! There was love everyplace. I felt the love from the
people in line with me, and I loved them too. I sensed the
love from God and his Son.

Heaven is just love, plain and pure, something for us to enjoy forever and ever and ever.

Do you remember what I asked you to consider at the outset of this book? Do you have an answer? Will I see you at the gate?

I'll wait for you there. I can hardly wait to go back.

So, until we meet again, I leave you with the words of Christ, ending my own humble revelation with the parting words of his:

"Look, I am coming soon! My reward is with me, and I will give to each person according to what they have done. I am the Alpha and the Omega, the First and the Last, the Beginning and the End. . . .

"I, Jesus, have sent my angel to give you this testimony for the churches. I am the Root and the Offspring of David, and the bright Morning Star."

The Spirit and the bride say, "Come!" And let the one who hears say, "Come!" Let the one who is thirsty come; and let the one who wishes take the free gift of the water of life. . . .

He who testifies to these things says, "Yes, I am coming soon."

Amen. Come, Lord Jesus.

The grace of the Lord Jesus be with God's people. Amen. (Rev. 22:12–21)

Postscript

On December 19, 2011, Marv and I took his co-writer, Lorilee, out for lunch. We wanted to treat her, as well as see her one more time before we left for Arizona, where we had spent the last few winters.

She had one more piece of business for Marv: the dedication and acknowledgments for this book. She walked us through the process of writing those final details, assuring us this was the last book-related task for Marv to do until it was published.

Over chicken salad sandwiches, we dispatched with the business at hand and spent the remaining time together chitchatting, as we always did. Marv and I hugged Lorilee goodbye, and we all promised to keep in touch via email. Marv loved working on the book with Lorilee, but it was also a very difficult project as well. Talking about his heaven experience was emotional and draining for Marv, and working on the chapters about losing our baby son, William, and later, our son-in-law Steve were particularly wrenching.

I knew Marv was relieved to be done. He had faithfully completed the work which God sent him back from heaven to do. Now we could relax in Arizona, golfing and visiting with our friends.

Except God had other plans. Marv had returned to earth almost six years beforehand, and had dearly longed to go back every minute of those years. We didn't know it that day at Russ' Restaurant, but God knew: Marv's time on earth was almost up.

The next day, Marv was hospitalized for pneumonia, and we spent the week of Christmas in the hospital. He was released briefly, only to be readmitted within a couple of days. This time he had pneumonia in the other lung. Marv was very weak, and it was so difficult for me to watch him in such a state, but I fully expected him to spend no more than two or three days in the hospital. During that time, I received more than one hundred emails from friends and family, concerned about Marv. He was so loved on this earth, but so much more loved in heaven.

On January 9, I noticed that Marv was experiencing marked weakness on his left side and had difficulty speaking and gripping the doctors' hands. A "stat" CT scan revealed a blood clot in the right side of the brain. He was transferred to ICU.

Here's an excerpt from my email to family and friends on January 13:

Marv has come through some very difficult days. He was able to pull out the feeding tube on Wednesday night. That had to be reinserted today. Swallowing remains a major problem. The feeding tube is necessary to give him many meds and maintain nutrition. He knows me but remains very tired. The doctors have a major dilemma. They reintroduce the anticoagulants and worry about bleeding around the clot in the brain. Or they stop the anticoagulants and worry about another blood clot. He remains very ill and truly in God's hands.

Marv continued to get worse, and on January 18, I had to make the hardest decision of my life—to have Marv's feeding tube removed. Another email:

After many tears, prayers and questions, we decided to stop all medication, food and keep him comfortable with pain meds. . . . This has been such a difficult decision but I know Marv would not want to live this way. Those of you who have heard him speak about his trip to Heaven know how much he wants to go back. This time it will be a one-way trip.

So many friends and family visited Marv for the next three days, including his co-writer, Lorilee. With tears rolling down her face, she held his hands and told him those two angels were coming for him, again. "Will you wait for me at the gate?" she asked him. Marv was barely coherent or lucid, but we could both tell he said "yes."

Our children and grandchildren were able to express their deep love for Marv, one more time.

On January 21, 2012, at 6:15 in the evening, Marv flew back to heaven. I had sat by his bedside that day, doing all

I could to make him comfortable, and whispering words of devotion. I loved him with all my heart. I knew he was at the departure gate, waiting for the angels.

A friend had brought me the devotional *Jesus Calling*. That day's reading gave me profound comfort. I also read it to Marv in those final hours:

> I want you to be all mine. I am weaning you from all other dependencies, Your security rests in Me alone—not in other people, not in circumstances. Depending only on Me may feel like walking on a tight rope, but there is a safety net underneath: *the everlasting arms*. So don't be afraid of falling. Instead look ahead to Me. I am always before you, beckoning you on—one step at a time. *Neither height nor depth nor anything else in all creation can separate you from My loving Presence.**

That day, God beckoned his child Marv straight into his everlasting arms. My dear one was at rest, back where he so longed to go.

Did those same two angels pick him up this time?

Was Peter there to greet him this time, and if so, what words passed between them?

I don't know the answers to those questions. But I know he has been reunited joyfully with our son William John and with our beloved son-in-law Steve.

I know that no intangible doorway separates him this time from those he cherished: his parents, his grandparents, and many friends.

Marv was sent back to us because God told him, "I have more work for you to do."

* Sarah Young, *Jesus Calling* (Nashville: Thomas Nelson, 2004), 22.

I believe that work was, in large part, this book you hold in your hands, a book completed one day before my husband's health began to fail, and filled with love from Marv to you, the reader. Of course, it is filled, much more than we can imagine, with love from the God who sent his stubborn servant back to write it.

Marv's dearest hope was that many others would glimpse the peace and glory he experienced in heaven. "Heaven is just love, plain and pure, something for us to enjoy forever and ever and ever," he wrote in these pages. Marv is basking in that incomparable love today!

—Ruth Besteman,
Byron Center, Michigan,
May 9, 2012

Coauthor's Acknowledgments

To the following people, my abiding gratitude:
To my precious Guild: Ann Byle, Alison Hodgson, Angela Blyker, Cynthia Beach, Shelly Beach, Sharron Carrns, and Tracy Groot, for unending support and love. Jana Olberg for sharing your beloved Dagny with me. Tracey Bianchi, Pastor David Beelen, Jamie Young, Gordy Van Haitsma. My agent, Esther Fedorkevitch, who never gave up on this project, and who was so good to Marv and Ruth. My old and new friends at Baker Publishing: Dwight Baker, the sales, marketing, editorial, and publicity teams, and especially to the smart and skilled Vicki Crumpton, who chose this project over so many others.

To my family, my love and thanks: Linda Reimer; Ken and Linda Craker; my husband, Doyle, and children,

Jonah, Ezra, and Phoebe—it was my joy to share Marv's slice of heaven with the people I love most.

To Ruth Besteman: Thank you for your huge help in every aspect of this book. Marv and I couldn't have written it without your support, encouragement, savvy insight, medical knowledge, and great memory. I came to love you and Marv dearly.

And to Marv: Thanks so much for trusting me with your story. It is one of the great honors of my life to write this book with you. Thank you for embracing me like a family member, and for being so sweet and funny and open-minded through this whole process. I miss you, but I know you are shining like the sun right now, with your God and those you love. When I die, I know you will be there at the gate, waiting, with a big smile on your face, and probably a crack about the Red Wings beating the Jets. We'll have to wait and see. Until we meet again, my thanks and love.

—Lorilee Craker

Marv Besteman (1934–2012) was a graduate of Calvin College, a veteran of the US Army, and a retired bank president. He spoke frequently during his last few years of life about his experience of heaven. He and his wife, Ruth, are the parents of three children and the grandparents of four. Marv passed away in January of 2012, joyfully anticipating his return to heaven.

Lorilee Craker is the author of twelve books, including *Money Secrets of the Amish*, nominated for a 2012 Audie Award; *A Is for Atticus: Baby Names from Great Books*; and the *New York Times* bestseller *Through the Storm* with Lynne Spears. A native of Winnipeg, Manitoba, she lives with her family in Grand Rapids, Michigan, where she also moonlights as an entertainment reporter for the *Grand Rapids Press*.

TRUE STORIES OF HOPE AND PEACE AT THE END OF LIFE'S JOURNEY